A MOROCCAN JOURNEY

James Scanlan

For Lyra, for Big G

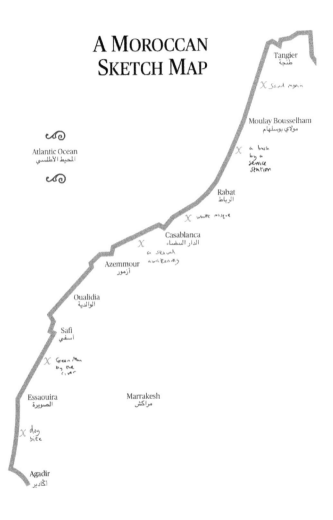

A MOROCCAN SKETCH MAP

Tangier
طنجة

X Saint marin

Moulay Bousselham
مولاي بوسلهام

X a bush
by a
service
station

Rabat
الرباط

X white mosque

Atlantic Ocean
المحيط الأطلسي

Casablanca
الدار البيضاء

X
المرصد a
awakening

Azemmour
أزمور

Oualidia
الوالدية

Safi
أسفي

X Green Man
by the
river

Essaouira
الصويرة

Marrakesh
مراكش

X dog
bite

Agadir
أكادير

Painted Lady Preface

There is a lady of the skies
A vagabond of butterflies

In springtime, from Moroccan sands
Her instinct longs for Angle lands

A rocky cycle leads her on
In tales of textures here and gone

The athlete artist's dappled stains
Of inkwell steps through nature's lanes

Until she rests in sunny parts
Alone the sum of all her hearts

A ribboned life's migration roots
Of broken generations' boots

Wayfarer fading born anew
On fairways to another who,

With candle burning for the greed
and dying for a freckled breed,

Knows the chrysalis so much more,
Than old ones on a distant shore,

That all this roaming relay brings
Is paint upon her canvas wings.

1

"The first question most travel writers feel they ought to deal with is 'why?' (Often the real reason is: to write a travel book. This is rarely admitted.)"

Tim Mackintosh-Smith (ed.), *The Travels of Ibn Battutah*

"WHERE ARE YOU STAYING IN MOROCCO?" demanded the officer. Muffled French behind the glass barrier at passport control. He wouldn't let me through without a fixed address. Panic. To be "fixed" was the exact opposite of what I intended. (Well, at least he hadn't asked, "why?")

Three days earlier, I'd left a job that had taken me to live in Egypt. Editorial training at a publishing house in Cairo. The prospect of promotion arrived on the same day, but I declined, deciding to walk home to England instead. Enough of pyramids and punctuation; I wanted adventure and anxiety. I wanted "what," not "why."

The following day I fell out with my landlord. And, in a fit of frustration—built up since an act of God had collapsed a mango tree onto my balcony (not, as was insisted, an act of James)—I stuck a frozen herring on top of a cupboard. Revenge would be slow, but the smell would linger. On the Saturday, I collected half my deposit (further disagreement about a broken washing machine, the herring still firm) and here I was on Sunday: impasse at Agadir airport.

I had been in Egypt for a year, variously compiling minutes of meetings and roaming between Citadel and Giza. However, I longed for wilder music and stronger wine. To be in nature at the mercy of time.

I wasn't bold enough to strike out through Libya to the west or Syria to the north, with ISIS at its peak and the borders closed. The story would have been more compelling, but I cared too much about seeing my family again. Eyes turned to Agadir, on the other side of Africa and, neatly, along the same latitude as Cairo. I'd form a line of passage and chase the curve north—coasting Morocco, across Spain and up France to Somerset.

In my bag, I packed various pieces of kit unworthy of a hashtag: sleeping bag, tent, spork etc. Plus all the cereal bars from my local supermarket. A host of miscellaneous items would turn up six months later at the bottom, crumpled, damp and important.

Friends gifted power banks and notebooks. I dressed in a green cap, a blue shirt, brown trousers and black trainers; all soon to be one shade of the same stale. Details felt important—looking the part is half the game. Though when it comes to preparation, I'd rather read about someone else's socks and make holes in mine. A flâneur not a plânner.

A few weeks before leaving, as I floated along the Nile on a boat crowded in neon, an Englishman explained that what my walk needed was a theme. This troubled me at the time, troubled me throughout and still troubles me now. As we drifted under the lions of Qasr El Nil bridge, he stood up to take a piss off the prow. Much to the surprise of the pilot and the couples entwined by the railings. I saw his point; I suppose we all did.

While he was busy leaking grand analogies of a hybrid *Zen and the Art of Motorcycle Maintenance* meets *The Alchemist* sort, I sank even further into a personal crisis that sought anything other than to be grand. I wanted to walk for the sake of walking. Yes, the next few months would often be uncomfortable, but I wasn't expecting to reach nirvana through my blisters. I just wanted to reach home, on foot.

I'm not immune to delusions of grandeur (see introductory poem above and forthcoming explanation). My urinating philosopher, who caused me much lingering existential questioning over the past few years, eventually fermented into the shape of a butterfly. A painted lady butterfly, to be precise, whose migration path just so happens to mirror the route that I would tread.

It's a path that may be taken as a long hop or a journey marked with a succession of generational stops and starts, the pied beauty reaching England is a descendant of the insect leaving Morocco. Each generation's wave has its story to tell, like the dots amassed on the individual's wings. Telling any of these tales, says old butterfly gramps to indifferent butterfly junior, is equal to telling the whole. And for the sake of these pages and the man on the boat, in my beginning, I've since determined, was my whole.

Lest I get spirited away by post hoc armchair lepidoptery, for me, the dots were language. I'd studied Arabic on paper, but I never learnt so much as when on the move. Language is living, so you might as well live it. I picked two marks on the map—separated and united by vernaculars, histories, cultures (and, ahem, butterflies)—and walked between them. Liberation in a journey that makes no objective sense.

Well, if, say, a chap from Agadir rolled out of bed two centuries ago with a sudden and inexplicable urge for a cream tea, what route would he have taken? (Five-minute reading ban if you said "boat"). Facetious, yes, but there's the point—an excuse to get out the door where the interesting things happen.

The artist Richard Long once walked 121 miles from the mouth of the river Loire until the first cloud he saw. A microadventure mentality. Or, at the very least, a nimbus disposition. This chair of butterfly whimsy sure is snug. (A conspiracy! Since the Arabic for "butterfly" shares the same root as that for "furniture.")

I'd stick to the old ways in the margins of asphalt and the footsteps of shepherds and pilgrims. I'd trace a network of hosts, chance encounters and friends. I was driven to find the interesting in the everyday and to share a daily blog as my incentive. (That is: to write a travel book.)

And just as the Arabic for "language" is etymologically linked with the word for "nonsense," I sought comfort from the maps in limericks:

There once was a man with a tent,

In Cairo, he lived and was bent

On doing a trek

'N to say, "Oh heck,

'Tis cheaper than a few months' rent."

But rhyme is no remedy for wrenching goodbyes. Her name was Shoroq. I'd taken the flat below her, and we'd sidled along throughout the year. The shade of a chanced love met the previous Autumn that was fated to simmer beyond the gaze of prying eyes. In the Spring, we set out on a walk to Alexandria, sleeping in mosques and sipping tea with mint pickers. The police stopped our jolly ("security," they'd said), and by the following Autumn, other differences put an end to the rest (we'd said.)

Stroll the Nile, hold hands at bus stops and argue about universal wossnames over mango juice. The thrill of spontaneity along that road to Alexandria sparked the desire for something grander. Her name means "sunrise," and as I boarded the plane under a pink dawn, my mind was a flurry of futures.

—

Overcoming the stalemate at Agadir airport was simple in the end, as most travel is nowadays despite what the vloggers insist. I'd arranged via Couchsurfing to stay my first night with a student called Yassir. I rang his number and handed the phone to the officer. Meanwhile, a policeman came to see what all the fuss was about and o my intentions tumbled out. We shook hands, "Walking to Tangier, eh?" he said, "what a superb idea!" and there followed much theatrics of his past as a champion runner. I jotted down Yassir's address as a record of an apparent residence and left the rest to the wind.

Yassir found me by a bush outside a hardware store in an eastern suburb. Dressed in fluorescent sports gear and a big sports watch, his hair gelled up in a quiff. Reminiscent of a 14-year-old version of myself: keen, serious and anxious. Exactly how I felt then as a gawkish 27-year-old. His family welcomed me into their home as if I were a distant cousin who's stopped in from Cairo for tea.

Out came the map, unfurled across a table in the aftermath of chicken, and I traced the route to Tangier with an index finger covered in rice. I had no exact idea of my route, but you can't get more precise than a coastline. Together we huddled over a paper Morocco under a tray of mint tea and biscuits shaped like a zero.

"We invented that," said Yassir's dad holding up a biscuit with a triumphant grin. By "we" he meant—perhaps inspired by the international nature of our huddle—various mathematicians from India. By "that" he meant the "zero." (By "holding" I mean the biscuit.) Yassir's dad and little brother (all in matching tracksuits) pored over every detail and pointed out certain caves in the south for me to visit. These were all in the opposite direction to where I was headed. The trip didn't compute despite their passion for maths.

Yassir's little brother sat in the corner, giggling and correcting his dad's French. A discussion ensued about whether Yassir should accompany me to Tangier. "To improve your English," said dad. Already feeling quixotic about the journey, I hadn't expected to have a Sancho thrust upon me so early. But Yassir was about to start his first year at university, so he concluded he had little time for anglophone hiking projects.

That evening, Yassir and I went for a look about town through fruit markets that tumbled to the corniche of bright lights and dull entertainment. Coming from a chaos of Cairo, the rambling carts and mere trickle of passersby felt sedate, almost orderly, among the sprawling modernist concrete. "God, Homeland, King" written large in Arabic stones below the kasbah on the pointed hill at the far end.

I stocked up with water, bread, cheese and dates for the first days and bought a sim card by a memorial to the 1960 earthquake, which completely levelled the area. Agadir is a city reborn, a place for new beginnings if ever there was one. Where only the rocks remain. We rode back to the suburbs in a cracked and crowded bus. And the sim card never worked.

At dawn, Yassir armed me with a bag of croissants and a tiny Moroccan slipper on a keyring—his tokens for my safe travel. We'd agreed the previous night that he'd join me on the first day. Though, waking in the dark, he found the prospect of a 9 am lecture far more appealing. So it was that I set off alone on my grand old adventure to England from a grand old crossroads of rubbish skips.

2

"Look! Don't you worry too much about me, Lewis. If by any chance things become a bit too strenuous in the ascent, I shall stop periodically and pant, all right?"

Colin Dexter, *The Jewel That Was Ours*

YOU'LL FIT IN SEAMLESSLY, he told himself, what with the shirt collar and the new pleats. But the heavy bag made a sweaty mess of his first traveller's commute. Within half an hour, the intrepid adventurer had become a drenched beacon among the suits and school kids of the Agadir rush hour. He stopped at the beach to rehydrate by the first Ferris Wheel to be built in Africa, he then readjusted pronouns and I walked off into a world of salty dizziness. The road climbed out of Agadir past a mass of industry and the world smelled of rotten fish. A toothless man on a scooter waved so vigorously that he wobbled and almost fell off.

I'd been increasingly troubled that foreigners wouldn't be allowed to walk alone in Morocco.

Fears ingrained from my experience in Egypt, where our walk to Alexandria had been curtailed by a lack of official "authorisation" (plus suspicions as to why a veiled Egyptian woman was leading a foreign man along a dark road: "Are you *convinced* by what you're doing?" had been the policeman's line).

But, now in Morocco, at the first traffic checkpoint after Agadir, I was neither arrested nor spoken to. Indeed, nobody took any notice at all. Thus convinced by my anonymity, I relaxed into a rhythm, chasing my morning shadow in the hard shoulder. Looping across the mouths of postcard bays: the deep blue of the ocean, the white horses a-leaping, the bright sand, the litter and the tarmac a-shimmering. By midday, I'd arrived at Aourir for my first nuss-nuss—"half-half." Espresso coffee poured into a glass of foamed milk, swirling into the fleeting shapes of a dairy jellyfish. A flowing jinn emerges to pronounce: "your caffeine is my command."

This first day was 30 kilometres to Taghazout, between asphalt and Atlantic. In a moment of inspiration infused with Google Maps and wishful thinking, I had assured my parents that I'd be home in three months and 3,000 kilometres, back in time for Christmas (surely!). After one day, I was on track. However, my estimations would be wrong by more than three months and over a thousand kilometres.

Shortly before Taghazout, the road reared up a sharp incline guarded by a man under a tree. He stood fanning himself with a bright orange EasyJet safety card. I addressed him a cheery "bonjour!" and he replied with an almighty "Bellissimo!" flourishing the lamination as if it contained some intrinsic universal significance.

We exchanged brief exclamations of safety, and he motioned to the fact that he was waiting for someone. A similarly lost air steward, presumably. And I hoped, even if everything crumbled in the coming months, I'd keep hold of more than the waterproof directions to a non-existent lifejacket.

He remained flapping in my wake as I strutted up then down into Taghazout, ignored the crowding touters and made for a "surfers" hostel. One salty bubble of a tajine later, I was reclining on the roof with a Moroccan worker from the hostel and talking to friends back in Egypt. They could barely understand one another's dialect but fared better in the register of high Arabic. And in the dreamy echo of a highfalutin air, I dropped into verse with a lute in a chair.

There once was a man with a flute,

On second thoughts, maybe a lute.

He'd sit in the yard,

While waving a card,

A confusion to all Taghazout.

The 19th-century Scottish weaver William McGonagall is generally regarded as the worst poet in the English language. In 1893, McGonagall wrote an angry poem threatening to leave his native Dundee. One newspaper joked that he'd probably stay for another year once he realised "that Dundee rhymes with 1893."

The doggerel doesn't improve much, but the dogs' grrs (sure as) 'el do. (And what of it?) I left Taghazout in the dark as the dawn congregation returned from the mosque. Three dogs interrupted their rummage through a skip to escort me. I out-marched them into a pink gloom, keen to trace some miles before the heat.

Sodden by the village of Imi Ouadar, I replenished with what would become my Moroccan staple: a few rounds of bread, one round of laughing cow cheese and a kilo of dates. And, just this once, a bag of zero biscuits (in honour of Yassir and global mathematics). Plus three one-litre bottles of water: one to fill my CamelBak (#SuckOnTheTruck), one as back up and the other I'd carry in my hands as a token of goodwill and hydration to any fellow pedestrians.

A path of stones around the headland and an immaculate swell to my left, where fishermen cast lines into the spaces between surfers. Becoming accustomed to the banal indignities of hiking and the acuteness of time when the world is on fire and everything hurts. The eternal specificity of gravel.

Groups of men huddled under lean-to shelters atop piles of discarded sardines. Assalamu 'alaykum, I would holler, to which they'd reply with a chorus of I-don't-know-what-exactly-but-it-didn't-sound-like-the-expected-wa-'alaykum-assalam-and-so-was-presumably-Berber, raising their right hands in a Mexican wave of peace.

I'd been assured that my spoken Arabic from Cairo would be widely understood thanks to the popularity of Egyptian films and music across the Arabic-speaking world. You can learn Berber (I'll come to this term) dialects, use some

French (Spanish in the North), English maybe, and gestures often. The Moroccan variety of Arabic (Darija) presents an onslaught of uninterrupted consonants to the uninitiated. And to the somewhat initiated, it's a confusion of scale where "whale" means "fish" and "house" means "bedroom."

The first, that "huut" is the Arabic term for "whale" (mostly) everywhere apart from North Africa (from Morocco to Tunisia), where it simply means "fish," perhaps has more to say about the exaggerations of the fishermen than the generalisations of the lexicographers. The second, that "house" (bayt) is used for "bedroom," would, in just a few weeks, nearly be the cause of an unexpected sexual awakening. I felt for any Moroccans heading to Egypt, unaware that the local term for "underwear" (libaas) could be misconstrued as the Darija for "how are you?" (labaas). Those poor Egyptian taxi drivers, "I said *pyramids*, not pants!"

Writing from Tangier, the American author Paul Bowles called high Arabic the "dead language that refused to die." Teachers continue to insist on calling it Modern Standard Arabic. Though (mostly) standard and definitely Arabic, it is by no means modern. It's a language from the past wrenched into the present and dressed up in the underwear of unity.

It takes a lifetime to learn Arabic, and that's if you were born speaking it. With five years under my belt, the Moroccan dialect sounded like Arabic translated from Arabic to my infant's ear. Words or syllables struck a chord, yet the whole generally washed over in a rush of staccato syllables. There was much I felt I should understand, half words caught up in the tantalising melting pot of dialects somewhere up in someone's ether, but I'd frequently resign myself to silence—sukuun, in Arabic. A term which means not only "silence" but the absence of a vowel.

On my first evening, I'd learnt some basics from Yassir and managed to ask the price of a bottle of water—"shahaal l-ma?" And would soon be eating my first grilled whale with no great disaster. The other key word was "smeetu"—thingamajig. An essential piece of vocab for feigning understanding in any language (for, as long as you can point and know a few verbs, it eliminates the need for nouns).

—

Around midmorning, in the village of Tiguert, I woke a man slumped on a chair outside a small shop for a coffee. He brought me a sachet of Nescafé. I suggested hot water, to which he merely tugged at his henna-dyed beard. I made do with an iced can of coke, and we sat together in the absence of a vowel as th dy hmmd. I took my leave and he snored on in peace.

A cool sea mist lay across the road by the lighthouse at the cape known as Ra's Ghayr—Arabic for "different head." A sudden eruption of barking in a blaze of dog. A shepherd—ensconced in vapours among his goats—murmured an apology with a lob of stones, which sent the dog chasing after him instead.

This lighthouse features in the final scene of the 2017 Moroccan film *Hayat* (Life), about a bus journey from Tangier to Agadir. It's a caricature of Morocco, from the religious conservative to the smokey musician, the prostitute to the exiled poet. In the end, I could've just watched the film, in reverse. But there's nothing quite like cracking your own ankles on the road, going forwards. Somehow, it's both worse and more beautiful, as I would gradually discover. Besides, the film ends in a car crash.

—

Always carry a stick—that's the general wisdom when hiking in foreign lands. To relieve pressure on the joints and to fend off animals. (And to look like a proper adventurer for the inevitable cover photo (no, that's not me on the cover (he's coming up in Chapter 4 (how exciting!))).) I'd heard but hadn't listened, having done most of my preparations at a squint through a haze of limericks. Now, under the spaced eye of the shepherd trying to placate the dog by hiding behind a goat, I fashioned a stick from a reed and strode on. It broke after a couple of strides, and by way of a postscript, the back of my right shoe fell out.

I'd read all the requisite tales of bohemian trampings across deserts, up continents and down rivers. Poetic descriptions and the thrill of the narrative spoke louder than the finer footnote details of such trips. Cautious of the hyperbole that comes with encountering the authentic. I had a brace of power banks to keep me charged until the end of days, but my shoes had been well worn over the year, with holes in the soles and gaps in the ankles. Anxious to start, I'd overlooked the importance of feet in favour of photos.

I needed another head. Collapsed in the cover of a tree, all scorn for the fields of deep green bursting with banana and marrow. The village of Tamri loomed lazy beyond the plenty, nestled at the end of this fertile valley.

It took several hours to drag myself along the last stretch inland. I was drawn by fading light (and raw hips and creaking feet) to a guesthouse that was somewhat more expensive than I'd hoped because, tired and stubborn, I refused to admit to the owner that I understood what he was saying. He likely assumed a hallucinating Frenchman had wandered, wallet first, into his midst. When I did find energy enough to argue the fee, thus betraying my understanding of his marginal comments in French about my appearance, the price instantly fell.

After a nap, I shuffled into town, bought a kilo of bananas like swollen, jaundiced hands, and then sat at a café in front of a blue and white mosque to listen to the talk of Tamri. Two at an adjacent table, sensing my foreign air, introduced themselves as Rasheed and Ibrahim, fisherman-surfers by trade.

"You'd better watch out telling a Moroccan you're heading to Essaouira," said Ibrahim, leaning in, "it means only one thing: you're looking for prostitutes."

This wouldn't be my last encounter with Morocco's reputation for rampant sex tourism. Rasheed invited me to spend the night together in his cave above the beach. I declined as graciously as I could, leaving the cogs of a plot to whir off in his mind. I took my yellow fingers to bed as the sun finally dipped below the orange hills of the banana valley.

The morning came in a blessing of mint tea and a pile of bread and honey. Unable to flex a swollen ankle, I folded a pair of socks in my shoes for support, then was off, a fresh bag of bananas swinging from my shoulders. The luscious plantations of Tamri were covered in a thin mist as I climbed out of the valley into the habitual pink of the day. Several women in yellow djellaba robes watched me pass with their pointed hoods, peaks of colour in the dust.

Jumping into ditches by the hard shoulder to avoid coaches. No shade. The sun had long drawn any thoughts from my head. I sheltered from the fiery rays in a drain hole until a dog appeared, and I was back on my feet in the twitch of an ear. A sudden series of sharp switchbacks launched an imposing hill where the coastline jolted abruptly into cliffs. High tide concealed romantic notions of strolling barefoot along undisrupted sands to Tangier.

I improvised a path up and over between dry fields of dry stones and discarded (and, thankfully, dry) nappies, and through villages of no more than a few dry chickens. Men on donkeys waved sticks as they trotted by—the joy of being uninteresting in a scenery full of interest. A hare, the size of a small dog, shot out from a pile of rocks. A scorpion reared up, and I crunched on with a sting in my step. The wild gallivant ended at the top of a narrow gulley, a cascade of rocks, and I scrambled back down to the tarmac.

Five hours later, my ankle was a complete mess. I hobbled into a village called Assaka to a chorus of "bonjour monsieur" from a group of schoolboys lined up outside the mosque. Uninteresting no longer. A row of French camper vans lurked nearby, their occupants avoiding my deranged smile, which screamed: "yes, I've out-touristed you, bitches."

I made straight for the mahlaba—a common feature of the landscape whose name is akin to "the place of dairy products" but is essentially a corner shop-cum-café, albeit with a bent for dairy. The Moroccan traveller's whey station. I lost myself in the swirl of a nuss-nuss, with socks off and a hunk of cheese on a circle of crust.

The mosque boys sat in the corner sucking ice lollies and watching in silence— entertainment in a man with salt-stained trousers. Eventually, I went to the counter to pay up and ask about the route to Imsouane. The man returned an expression of concern and called over a young boy—the nominated French speaker of the mahlaba—who brought the crowd with him to see what old salt knees wanted.

The area's cut with deep gorges, he said, impossible to reach the sea. The only route to Imsouane would be the main road, take a left, then down the cliffs. I thanked the boys, who scurried back to their lollies. The man at the counter wished me well, and there was a collective wince as I settled my bag over a towel wrapped around my hips and proceeded to fall to the bottom of the steps.

Hours later, I was shuffling through the outskirts of self-pity when a van came zooming past and screeched to a halt. A tangle of beach-blonde locks dangled out the window:

"Fancy a ride, buddy?"

"How far to go?"

"Oh, like eight Ks, mate! Not Far!"

Was this it, then? Failure so early. Failure of what, though? I didn't have a theme or a point, and I wasn't a butterfly; I was heading home. Matters of pride didn't bother me at the time, revelling in uncertainty. I grumbled and got in the van.

In retrospect, I wasn't yet in shape to walk 10 hours a day with a heavy pack and swollen feet, attempt to make friends into the night, and then do it all again after a few hours of sleep. The sum of my preparation in Cairo involved sun salutations on the balcony (mainly for the enjoyment of giving the older man in the flat opposite the willies). Yoga on the roof, then acclimatise on the hoof. Was this a journey of discovery? Perhaps, but of other people, not the breaking point of my ankles.

Or, rather, that the pen is mightier than the crutch.

I rode with a group of excitable Polish surfers who'd driven from Portugal to run a surf camp. We stopped for photos at the first sighting of Imsouane, far below on a spit of land curving into the Atlantic like its coveted prized wave. Two Moroccan boys came to beg for money, and the Poles swore at them and drove on in high spirits. The whole episode was regretful.

My host was Sally, a former estate agent from England and her house in warm surroundings of today's bottles and yesterday's hashish. Cosy, homely and, most importantly, horizontal. I lay on the beach by sunset, the day's pains ebbing away as a cool mist rolled in with the last of the longboarders.

Time to recoup for this bold adventurer. Less Paul Theroux and "the inspired man's way of heading home," more James Scanlan and the insipid man's way of making more out of what was, so far, only a three-day walk than is probably necessary. But what do you expect if I started with an allegory about butterflies? Never fear; in the next chapter, there be wild dogs.

3

"Readers would stay to find out whether the pig mentioned in the opening paragraph would reappear as a significant part of the story."

Steve Aylett, *Lint: The Incredible Career of Cult Author Jeff Lint*

PAUL THEROUX, IN *THE TAO OF TRAVEL*, advises the traveller to read a novel that has no relation to the place they are in. Perhaps the above *Lint* was a step too far—it's the fictitious biography of a fictional author of such disparate clauses as: "Ambiguity is what a dog leaves behind when it gets in the car." Yet losing yourself in your own (or someone else's) idiosyncrasies can be comforting when you're alone and dehydrated. Besides, "a step too far" was very much the idea. Theroux says to let the influence of travel flow in reverse. To be informed and inspired by your direct experience. Rather than by someone else's honed and hastily Wikipedia-ed prose about the place. It's far better than forcing feelings for sights and sounds that once were but are no more. I'm not sure about pigs, but I do recall a mention of butterflies.

—

Imsouane is a Berber (Amazigh) fishing port at the foot of a high wall of cliffs. The men fish, work in the cafés and hostels or teach surfing, and in the evening, play cards and watch football in a crowded room down a narrow alley. I was told the women live in the next village, beyond the booze shop.

"Berber" is a controversial term, "a word which in Arabic as in the European languages has the ring of 'barbarian'," says the Arabist Tim Mackintosh-Smith. It is nonetheless the term that all "Berbers" I met would use to describe themselves when speaking French and English. Most likely because it's the term they expected I'd be familiar with. In Arabic, you hear the names of the various peoples, cultures and dialects that weave a vast network of Tamazgha to the Siwa Oasis in northern Egypt. Whether Amazigh and Imazighen, the "free people," or Tamazight, the language and its numerous dialects from Soussia in the Agadir region to Riffian in the north.

Sally introduced me, one evening, to Walid, who set to work on my ankle with warm argan oil as I shovelled down omelette after coffee. He smoothed out bumps and pulled things until they popped. "Berber massage," he reassured me, and I heard the "barbarian" ring through the pops.

I lounged alone for the day amongst generations of French couples and harbour sorts who hang around the ports a lot, like the brace of surfer-poet Bristolians who materialised in a café citing a Facebook post and an aunt who'd heard of my walk.

I'd been feeling quite the fraud so far, more than happy to slip unseen among the Atlantic tourists. This meeting brought a certain spring to my limp. Josh, Louis and I enjoyed an evening of small-world talk over large-world tajines by the fishing boats. I went to bed emboldened by the prospect of my future steps, to walk with pride, and to get more dirt on my Oxford shirt.

Lurking beneath Imsouane's hippy veneer is the sense of a less flowery truth. The divide between the tourists and the workforce is as clear as between the hostels and the card rooms. Sally had first come to Imsouane on holiday and then decided to make a go of it in the tourism industry.

However, only a few months later, she was forced to leave, by which time I was shivering somewhere in central Spain. Something about death threats from locals who owed her money. Perhaps there's a much deeper point here about infrastructure, relative wealth and privilege. Whatever was going on, I vowed to get my ankles out of town the next day.

I snuck off before sunrise along a dust track carrying a pink paper bag of bananas and peaches. Eyes peeled for ambiguity. I marched in the shade of the cliffs. Here and there, the rock opened up, revealing steep-sided valleys rich with green and graded farmland. Palm trees swayed, and a lone donkey lingered, laden with crops and awaiting orders.

I was heading inland, now, up slopes through villages where colourful school walls were the only excitement. Past a row of drab box buildings at Timizguida Ouftas, to the unambiguous "Maqha Isbania" (Café Spain), or so was written on the side of a squat house. I'm heading for Spain, wanted tea and could always do with a squat, so in I wafted.

After a few false starts, I eventually understood the owner, Abdulrahman, and his "wesh beeti?" (one way of saying "what do you want?" in Darija). He showed me to a chair and turned on the TV. Arsenal was playing, which, judging from the encouraging glances, I was supposed to find homely or, at the very least, significant. Abdulrahman brought over mint tea, bread and a small pot of argan oil and sat at my side. We slurped (sweet and cleansing) and devoured the soft bread dipped in rich and nutty oil. I learnt the Soussia word for delicious—ifolki.

Several hours over several pots of tea, in the calm among the activity of other people. Watching the morning stock take of carrots, tomatoes and grapes the size of eyeballs. An old boy squatting in the corner noted weights and barked commands. Each crate heaved onto a set of scales and then stacked on a truck bound for the markets back in Agadir. With their produce unloaded and their morning's work done, the men sat down with tea. To exist in silence just for a moment. Every so often, a bell rang on the far side, and Abdulrahman ran over to open a shutter and hand a bag of bread to the woman who had rung.

Most of those I met along this stretch of coast struggled with my Egyptian Arabic, though being Muslims, they generally understood my low utterances in the high language. But Abdulrahman insisted on finding a French speaker and nominated Mohanad, a bus driver just back from dropping the village kids off at school. Thus, and perhaps inspired by an audience, I explained to the gathered men that I was walking to England. Then quickly changed to Tangier when I noticed their eyebrows sliding off in bafflement. Nevertheless, this still provoked a flurry of questions: You don't have a job? Where's your family? Are you married? Your poor mother! I narrowed my focus further and settled for an exaggeration:

"You know Ibn Battutah?" I said to general excited nodding, then, "Well, I'm his son, Ibn Ibn Battutah!"

A smattering of chuckles rippled along the cheap seats despite the fact it doesn't really make sense in Arabic, but I nevertheless made a note to use it again. Why might this be so hilarious? I hear you groan. Ibn Battutah (meaning "the son of Battutah") was a native of Tangier who, in the 14th century, travelled for 29 years between Morocco and China. He set off the year after Marco Polo died and travelled further and wider in both extent and time than his Venetian counterpart.

At 21, Ibn Battutah left his home on the pilgrimage to Mecca. But, in that great gap-year tradition, he ended up overshooting by several continents and several decades (and fathering about ten sons along the way). He had been spurred on, he insisted, after an encounter with an Egyptian mystic who told him to send his regards to his fellows in Sindh, India and China.

His wonderings had been foretold—how very handy. ("Mum, met a shaman [wizard emoji], I'll be back in thirty years [ship emoji, globe emoji], IB xx.") It wasn't about firsts; it was travel, not exploration (with flurries of polygamy). And as travel goes, it was travel as life. (Albeit a life of leaving behind a wake of progeny and concubines to struggle in the hope that royalties from the inevitable book deal might one day trickle down.)

Ibn Battutah eventually returned to Morocco, where he retired to regional obscurity, and a scribe called Ibn Juzayy was given the daunting task of compiling his recollections. The result is perhaps the most extensive travel account (and, some have argued, most long-winded) ever written—A Gift to Those Who Contemplate the Wonders of Cities and the Marvels of Travelling.

A dubious (and, according to many aggrieved online sources, fabricated) saying of the

Prophet Muhammad instructs Muslims to seek knowledge even if they have to search as far as China. (The sentiment holds nonetheless; when has truth ever got in the way of advice.) Ibn Battutah took this literally (though he didn't like what he found there). Today, any mention of his name across the Arabic-speaking world brings with it a recognition of travel and knowledge-seeking. Even among the trendies who contemplate frappuccinos at the lavish Ibn Battuta shopping mall in Dubai: a city that leans so much on its presumed wonders that it hasn't noticed the marvels upped and travelled long ago.

—

When I stood to leave, Abdulrahman filled my water, brought me bread, refused my money (I left it, clumsily, all the same) and insisted on a photo. I still hadn't decided where I was headed that day, and Abdulrahman suggested I could make it to the village of Tafedna before nightfall. However, estimations of its distance varied wildly among the men (three kilometres? fifteen?).

For the rest of the afternoon, I hugged a path along a sheer drop to the ocean. Low tide sands stretched for miles, and the odd fishing vessel bobbed in the surf. I longed to be down there, too, bobbing. Impossible lodges and shrines hid in the coves. What mystics dwelled down there?

Here I was, galumphing with the goats on the gravel. A man on a motorbike wearing a bucket for a helmet stopped and asked if I wanted a ride. Since my moment of weakness before Imsouane, I was determined to be made of stronger stuff, so I grudgingly declined, and his bewilderment was my reward. Besides, he only had one bucket.

Black-and-white squirrels skittered across walls, chased by a screaming billy. Ravens cawed along the thermals. Camels chewed on trees bent horizontal by the wind. Towards mid-afternoon, the unforgiving rocks became a bed of hot needles. I was reduced to resting on the cemented covers of drainage tunnels, spaced every hundred metres, to ease the throbbing for a few minutes. A man stood by a bend in the track and watched me approach in this fashion, and as soon as I was in range, he yelled for a cigarette.

I'd anticipated this and had a pack of Camels and a lighter. I'm not a smoker, but this is a tried and tested (though not #NHSapproved) way of endearing myself to (and, if necessary, placating) strangers. I asked of Tafedna, and he motioned vaguely behind him. Our conversation passed in a mash of dialects. He asked if I was Muslim, to which I shook my head, and he looked me over with a disapproving air heightened by the fact that he was leaning on a tall stick. I noticed that the drain cover beside me was adorned with a graffito of some relevance—a question mark. I sat against it with my back to him and stared at the horizon like a heathen.

I left him to his stick and limited vowels and soon arrived in the bay of Tafedna, where I side-stepped a bucking horse and took a top bunk at the Green Donkey lodge—stocked full of twenty-something European drifters (ahem). It was cold showers, candlelit dinners and frogs in the drains. If I'd arrived under other circumstances, I would've fallen in love with any number of people there. But as it was, I think I just smiled for a few hours before hobbling to bed, suddenly struck by my own absence of vowels.

Across from me, as I lay down to sleep, a quote of (apparent) surf philosophy was plastered on a wall: "You never actually own a wave, but those who ride her are never forgotten." I understand it even less now than I didn't understand it then and spasmed throughout the night like a dog chasing pretentious surfer rabbits in its sleep.

—

Robert Louis Stevenson said the following on dogs: "He represents the sedentary and respectable world in its most hostile form...and if he were not amenable to stones, the boldest man would shrink from travelling afoot." If only I'd read this the night before rather than musings on the metaphysical implications of sex wax.

It was pitch black when I dropped from the bunk. Dead feet pleaded for the warm bed, but adventurers must be steadfast. I dodged the croaks to splash some stiffness into my upper lip and hit the road under a red sky full of omens. I'd picked a route that appeared to weave for an indeterminable distance to some other road I could follow to Sidi Kaouki. Up and over undulating hills covered in loose rocks, argan trees and herds of hobbled camels. Some of the stones hissed, and on closer inspection, they were tortoises.

Intermittent lone men were engaged in various pursuits among the trees: digging holes, staring at goats or stuffing argan into the saddlebags of indifferent donkeys. They would invariably approach and motion for a cigarette. None spoke French and only vaguely understood my Arabic, and all I could say in the local dialect of Tamazight was "delicious." We exchanged tastes of the day through hand signals, raised eyebrows and puffed-up cheeks.

It rained heavily all morning, with frequent forays from lightning and thunder. I wasn't yet drilled in donning my waterproofs (stuffed at the bottom of my bag, filed away under Probably Won't Need Till Europe), so I sat out the downpours under low canopies. Quite risqué, what with the lightning—I do have my moments. And was soon to have another.

Sometime after midday, I was cresting a hill in the perfection of blankness, and the world was a vivid whiff in the post-rain petrichor. I'd been listening to a Douglas Adams audiobook to ease the existential blues and was now in the post-Adams glow of seeing everything as wonderfully exciting and delightfully silly. Then, with no sound, warning, or notice put up in the basement of a local planning office, three dogs appeared from the dust, racing hard with their snouts low to the ground. Two split off for the flanks, and the leader bared its teeth. It edged in, growling, and then bit my shin before I could say "rabies." I instinctively kicked out and was rewarded with another nip to the right foot. The two behind snarled ever closer. I was transfixed by the snapping, slavering canines to the front, forcing me to retreat into the jaws of the others. I turned this way and that, surrounded by dog and consumed with horror.

A handful of stones in my pocket for just such an occasion but, in the moment, I feared being bitten again were I to reach down. The idiot, I wasn't carrying a stick. Unable even to proffer a cigarette. Instead, I twisted and shouted, loud and rather feebly.

Then came a rush of shrieks, and a volley of stones rained down from the trees. Two women in long, pink hooded djellabas came sprinting in a flurry of colour and garbs, screaming until the dogs scurried away to the herd of goats I hadn't noticed grazing in the nearby trees. I collapsed on the track in shock, shaking. The women were extremely agitated and fussed over the bloodied rip in my trousers. All I could do was apologise—the dogs were, after all, only doing their job. "I'm so sorry, brother," the older of the two kept saying.

My anger was with myself. I thanked them but refused their help and walked over the brow of the next hill to slump against a tree and clean and dress the wound alone. Damned devotion to duty for duty's sake. Mostly Harmless, my arse. Although the dogs hadn't been wild (and I'd had my jabs before coming), I erred on the side of caution and decided to make for a hospital. A British traveller had just that month been bitten by a cat in Morocco, contracted rabies and died.

The closest hospital was a day away in Essaouira, and the nearest taxis would be in Sidi Kaouki, around 23 kilometres away. A distance which then seemed like the end of the universe. But I had no option, and there was no way I was hitchhiking (I'd developed a gloriously carefree, yet potentially detrimental, streak of stubbornness).

Fortune had it that in 2013 I'd spent three months volunteering on a farm to the north of Sidi Kaouki. A period spent digging holes, harvesting argan and nursing a prolonged bout of diarrhoea. Character building, at times lonely and others dehydrating, but in the end, possibly lifesaving.

I covered the distance to Sidi Kaouki in four blurred hours with a quiver of stones at the ready, arriving in the late afternoon with a fresh brace of blisters. An overpriced taxi to A&E in Essaouira later, the guard at the gate inspected the rip in my trousers and told me I should probably see someone about it. Such was the triage system. The doctor sighed as I sat down, "You look awful," he said, then plunged a succession of needles into my arm.

The sky over the old medina was a vivid crimson as I emerged, dejected yet relieved. I walked back through streets I already knew to a hostel full of people I didn't want to, trying not to dwell on the best-laid plans of dogs and men.

—

"Often windblown, generally delightful," such was Essaouira for Charles Payton, the British Consul here in the 1880s, "a land where it is always afternoon." He obviously hadn't heard of the prostitutes. Named "Tassort" in Tamazight, "Mogador" by the Portuguese in the 16th century and in Darija, "Souira" (which means "a small fort" and is perhaps a jibe at the stature of the Portuguese ramparts). In 1969, Jimi Hendrix lived here for three weeks in a derelict shack on the far side of the beach, or so herbally-inspired locals will insist to anyone who looks remotely in need of a camel ride.

In the past few centuries, Essaouira boasted a sizeable Jewish population consisting mainly of Brits from Gibraltar wearing bowler hats made in Manchester. So much so that it was said that "the cafés lilted with English accents." My taxi driver from Sidi Kaouki had talked with great pride about how he was descended from Amazigh Jews, "which is where I get my shrewd business sense from," he said. I reflected on this truth as I withdrew a fresh wad of cash to replace yesterday's fare.

I spent one day shuffling between cafés that now lilt with Californian accents among the twin aromas of sweet mint and rotting meat. I made a determined mess at mending my trousers with needle and thread and bought a wooden cane and a couple of pairs of socks.

And then I spent a few more days watching my socks drip from the top bunk among the general saccharine surrounds of travelling "someday" sets. "Someday, darling," came an excruciatingly elongated English accent through the window, "I'm going to pen a sonnet that will save the world." Pen—urgh. However, I may have been delirious and/or dreaming. I ventured out in the evening for a hearty chickpea and lentil soup (the traditional Moroccan comfort broth called harira), and the town was consumed in thick fog—a right (chick)pea souper. The mist of nonsense verse descended once again:

There was an old poet from Kaouki,

Who had a slight scare of the rabies.

"Why haven't we seen

Your verse on the screen?"

"'Cos most of my poetry's foamy."

The next morning, I was the first at the Bureau Municipal d'Hygiene for two further jabs in each shoulder. And I would need two more over the month, so I had to plan my route accordingly. The next town along the coast with a vaccine clinic was Safi, 124 kilometres away. A five-day pootle to meet my next needle.

Besides, if I had to listen to one more wailing rendition of *Knockin' on Heaven's Door* from the hostel's resident minstrel, I'd open the door and knock him in myself. But first, to make up for the unplanned sojourn in Essaouira.

I woke at dawn with the muezzin in the midst of a vocal warm-up before the call to prayer, which, when he reached it, was drowned out by a cockerel. The streets were empty but for cats and obscured by another chickpea souper that would last until noon.

I made for Bab Doukala at the northern gate of the old medina. A group of men was gathered around a small room in a yawning huddle of steaming cups, milky coffee and thin slices of cake. One man stood behind a neat row of glasses, two sugar cubes waiting in each. His woollen hat resting on large, protruding ears, sleeves rolled up under an oversized vest, and hands and mouth shaking with the effort. He poured a continuous stream of coffee as the men passed through, and not a drop spilt. I joined the shuffle, collected my coffee and cake, sat on the kerb waiting for the first bus, and listened to a street sweeper berate his colleague for pissing outside a public toilet.

Sidi Kaouki, when we arrived, was a wild dog convention. I hurried back down the road picking up stones as I went, and took an inspired left that found me on a dirt track and in an arena with four more dogs. I launched a pre-emptive broadside, which kept them at bay, barking like so many broken toys until I was out of sight.

Next, a line of camels in the distance lolled like ships on the horizon, shepherded from behind by a motorbike. I sat against a tree and waited for the caravan to pass. The shepherd was interested to know where I'd walked from, where I was going, and if I had somewhere to stay when I arrived. He asked if I was Egyptian, and I said no but quietly glowed. He said something about not wanting to lose his camels, got back on his bike and shot off after the herd. Over the engine revs, I made out his parting words: "Auf Wiedersehen!" My glow was snuffed.

Barefoot along the long beach to the port at Essaouira. A crowd of cameras lurched behind three sharks being dragged by their flapping tails to meet the great fishmonger in the sky. I celebrated the end of my first week with a fresh orange juice whilst trying to come up with a fresh limerick about an old man from Kaouki who lived by the quay and found a portkey to a room that was pokey..., but in this, I failed, became derailed then just sat there all mopey. Or something to that effect. Dog bites and so forth. At least now I was ready to leave the land of wind and eternal afternoons, armed with a stick and poorly sewn-up trousers. Often limping, generally hungry.

4

"Nobody cares that much. I'm sorry that's not true. Nobody cares at all."

Bill Bryson about people who blog when hiking

HE WAS REFERRING SPECIFICALLY to those who trek the Appalachian Trail—over 2,000 miles of witticisms about trees. But his point stands. It's difficult not to get drawn into ineffectual musings of ennui, incompetence, blisters and laments for the latrine. The simile comes later, if at all, and is frequently as desperate as the whole endeavour was in the first place. One week in, obstinacy had been my only obstacle. The prospect of untrodden sands lay ahead, and I fizzed with possibility like an (oh sod it) forward-thinking can of Fanta.

Back to Bab Doukala at dawn for coffee and cake. The crowd filtered through in silence under the arch of steam and sugar. On that bleary morning, I was no longer a strange spectacle despite my lumpy bag—just another cold human with a warm cup. I revelled for a moment in my newfound sense of being, then made off north along the sea wall. Not two steps later, I came across a group of teenagers on their way to school, pointing and giggling: "What are you, old?" they said. In response, I gave them a Chaplin twirl of my new stick and set off into the day with a giggle of my own.

The sky was a palette of the primaries as I reached the end of a run-down industrial terrace, picking out the finer aromas of ageing fish between the burnt plastic. I snuck out of town on a path of rubbish between warehouses and onto a broad expanse of sand. Finally, there it was, the Atlantic coastline laid bare before me.

It was a morning of clean walking on hard sand. The occasional fisherman stood by the shore, between a rod and a motorbike. Solitary dogs roamed the dunes. At one point, a waif in shorts hurried past, holding a long stick with a small crab bobbing from the end on a length of string. I watched him run into the distance, growing smaller for over an hour, and not once did he look back. Men and women were harvesting the rock pools for mussels; goats grazed on seaweed around them, and donkeys stood staring. As I neared my destination for that day, Moulay Bouzerktoun, a row of camels, crested the dunes to my right and stood perfectly silhouetted against the sky for a brief moment. It had been a glorious day of beach walking, and I arrived in the village positively buzzing with life and all the creatures in it.

The first person I encountered scowled at my cheery isn't-life-great-where's-the-nearest-café-squire?. I turned back a few steps later, and he was still gawping, half-obscured behind a wall. Something in me flipped, and I charged at him with my stick in the air until he shrieked and scurried away behind the boulders. It wasn't my finest interpersonal moment. Though, nor was it his.

I walked on into the most eerily empty Windsurfing Hub of International Repute I'd ever been to. Derelict former hostels boarded up and covered in graffiti, loose shutters clattering in the strong wind. A mass of surfboards by a door was the first sign of life. And there, in a courtyard, I met Soufian. He didn't bat an eyelid as I explained where I'd come from/was going/etc., just smiled and showed me to a bed in this (what turned out to be) surfers' retreat.

A storm raged all afternoon and evening. I lay on the sofa popping dates with three chain-smoking windsurfers from Switzerland, Sweden and Egypt. Frustration for them and satisfaction for me as we watched the seagulls suspended in the gales. My mind was spinning with thoughts of a distant home. The futures were limitless in that warm shelter.

During a brief break from the elements, I went out to buy bread and cheese. The shopkeeper handed me a complimentary bag of local sweet pastries and corrected my small-talk assertion that this was a lovely "Amazigh" village, "No, we are Arabs here," he said firmly. This was the only time I came across such sentiment in Morocco.

And a storm fired throughout the night.

A bank of cotton wool descended the cliffs towards the sea as I set off through the outer wastes at sunrise, past overflowing skips and a mosque above the sands. Two female dogs appeared almost immediately as I re-joined the beach and followed at a distance just outside stone-throwing range. I rolled with my bitches for an hour before they sulked off into the dunes without a nibble. Low tide exposed the shore— on one side, the endless breakers, and on the other, almost a mile of dunes stretching to a range of sloping hills.

The stroll was gentle this morning, and it took only a few hours to reach the sheltered bay of Bihbeh, a place impossible to pronounce with a complete set of teeth. (When asked about my trip over the coming weeks, I'd invariably cover up Bihbeh as an unexpected cough.)

Blue and red wooden fishing boats sat around the dark blue waters of the half-moon bay. I came to the only shop and, addressing it at large, asked where an itinerant European might rest his head for the night. The owner shrugged and suggested a can of coke instead. Then a man next to him in green swimming shorts, a blue t-shirt and a beige sun hat said simply "yes" and motioned for me to follow. He led me a short distance to a room by the edge of a small cliff. Inside was a large mattress, a hole in the floor, a gas stove and a sea view.

Abdulfatah was his name, or Agudor the Wise, as he'd later insist. I'd taken him for a tourist, what with the green swimming shorts and sun hat, but he was a bona fide fisherman from the neighbouring village of Aqermoud. This was his fishing lodge and a holiday let for summering Moroccans and, now, wintering Brits. I never did work out what "Agudor" meant. I couldn't understand much of what he said in Darija. His sympathy (for he understood

Egyptian and French but couldn't speak them) stretched as far as ending most sentences with: "It's difficult, right?" He was yet to stress his moniker: "The Wise."

I lay on a cushioned banquette watching the wise man slice up a bucket of octopus. In the other corner sat Amin, a rotund and bearded 26-year-old Qur'an teacher. Amin made us tea and reclined to smoke hashish from a thin wooden pipe called a sebsi.

"Are you married?" he asked, speaking a mishmash of Moroccan, Egyptian, coughs, Classical Arabic and French for my benefit, and I said I wasn't in a scramble of shrugs. Between the put-put hits of the pipe, Amin talked of his recent wedding: "It was simple. We just said prayers, no music or dancing like you have," he said, motioning at me with his pipe. To begin married life with the halal (permitted by Islam), not the haram (forbidden), he continued before leaning back against the wall, lighting up and singing *Knockin' on Heaven's Door*. Even Agudor, elbow-deep in octopus, looked up. There's nothing quite so energising as other people's hypocrisies.

Agudor (now installed as "The Wise") handed round freshly boiled crabs from a steaming pot. Both he and Amin cracked open the shells with their teeth and devoured theirs in an instant. I put mine to one side, with a half-nibbled leg, and wrote up my journal. Amin and Agudor played cards until the octopus was tender.

Over tentacles in a spicy tomato sauce, my anxiety turned to the next day's route. Looking at this stretch properly for the first time (rather than as yet another section in that Great Abstract that remained, to me, the Moroccan coastline), I noticed a river just before my planned destination of Souiria. And the only bridge was 12 kilometres upstream. That's quite a detour for a Jim on foot, and it would mean a big trek along the main inland road rather than a comparatively jolly stroll along the shore. Amin said the river would be too high to cross because of the recent rain. Agudor, who was now boiling a chicken whilst completing a crossword, tutted (wisely) and said it should be fine, knee-deep at most.

Perhaps they knew someone who lived there whom we could ring to find out? "No," Amin said flatly, "watch out for the people in the next town; they aren't as friendly as us." I'd heard this before, in Tamri, Imsouane and Essaouira. I'd heard it in all the "next towns" before this one. The pervading tendency to be wary of those from the north or, more precisely, in the next village. A mistrust that seeks to boost local bonds, possibly, while manifesting as a form of one-upmanship, maybe. Whatever it is, it's an impossible comment to counter as it strikes from the heart of contradiction. Thank God I'd arrived from the south.

Nonetheless, the matter was settled: another blissful day of sand, and the river would be whatever it would be. The remainder of the afternoon was spent in the twin fragrances of hashish and bubbling sea creatures.

I awoke in the dark with Amin standing over me in boxers and a head torch. "Come on, we're going fishing," he said. We scoffed some boiled chicken with onion and olives, turned on our lights, and made out into the night. We scrambled through a hole in a large rock called Jarf al-hammam ("the cliff of the toilet"). Above us, the stars and milky way outshone the crescent moon, and all along the shore, the torches of other parties darted about like fireflies. There were two skies that night as we crossed a vast tangle of deep rock pools and sharp edges over a charcoal gleam. The brief was simple: call out if you see any hint of tentacle or claw.

We bent low over the water, looking for a bulbous head or a wandering leg. I spotted an octopus in the first pool and called out. Amin lumbered over, yanked the tentacles in a swift jerk and dispatched the octopus with two wet, heavy thuds on the rock. He stuffed the limp creature in a bag over his shoulder, hitched up his pants and lumbered on.

At the next pool, I found two more and soon earned the title of mua'lim al-okhtobuut ("octopus master," or as I heard it (complete with capital letters) "Octopus Slayer") and, overcome with guilt, stopped pointing them out. Feigning interest in some barnacles, I began to lag behind the other two as their shoulder bags filled with the fruit of the hunt. "Hey, Octopus Slayer! Found any more?" Amin would shout. "Not a sausage!" I'd reply, sharing a glance with an eye or a claw among the seaweed. I soon returned alone and defeated, weaving through the flitter of torch beams and up the u-bend of toilet cliff to crash out until dawn, somewhere in the foothills of metaphor. Flushed out, this snowflake of the sea.

I was up early to find Agudor boiling a pot of water. All this man does is boil things. Maybe that's what "Agudor" means. To be wise, must one boil? We sat outside in the chilly morning air, drinking tea and eating bread smothered in butter melted on the gas burner. The sky in purples and blues, with the lingering crescent moon our vestige of the night's forage. He and Amin had returned from the rock pools with an impressive haul, indistinguishable from the mass of the heaving Amin by which it lay. Agudor shrugged off my thanks for his hospitality, saying, matter-of-factly, that I should get going before the tide turned. Twenty steps later, I was on the beach and away.

Sure enough, the tide came in soon after midday. It had been a blissful march over firm sands, in blue skies and rap battles with seagulls, but I was now forced up ever-diminishing pebbly slopes, and my feet roared. Souiria came into view beyond the mist, dots of white buildings, the blue of a corniche, the implication of a café. And there was the river; its banks long burst as the sea continued to flood.

I slumped to my feet, despondent. But I was so close to my destination that my mind was made up to cross. I stuffed all valuables into a dry sack, covered my bag in its waterproof and stripped to my boxers. It was around five metres wide, white crest hurdles on a bubbling current. Jumpable.

Then just as I took my first step, a voice yelled from behind. I turned to see a small man waving frantically from the dunes. I pulled up my trousers and went to see what he wanted. He introduced himself as Mohammed and told me in slow and deliberate French that I would be swept out to sea if I attempted to cross. I suggested he was overreacting and that I had a plan, waterproof bags, an inflated spirit of adventure etc. He listened patiently, then led me back down to the water's edge, where he stood with hands on hips:

"No, no, the tide's far too high. Come, drink some tea, wait for an hour, then try and cross." His gums whistled, and each clause ended with a wheeze I felt in my colon.

His elderly and skinny frame yet steady manner gave him the aura of a retired wood elf. Green, baggy and threadbare jumper, black suit trousers and leather shoes trodden down and worn for years as slippers. Through the general gauntness, his eyes glistened with a deeper understanding that was probably cataracts. He showed me to a tiny sticks-and-ropes shack on the dunes, rammed full of an assortment of fishing tackle. I nestled among the nets with my feet on a tyre and dozed off against a stiff wind.

"What am I? Nosing here, turning leaves over / Following a faint stain on the air to the river's edge." My weary mind had drifted until it met a future memory of these Ted Hughes lines, took an inspired left at folklore and, together with hindsight and reading, concluded al-Khidr ("The Green One")—Islam's "learned man at the junction of the two seas." Islamic spirit of nature and purveyor of wisdom to boot. And, by way of an encore, came his fanciful twinning with the Green Man, the Green Knight of Arthurian legend and even Shakespeare's Puck.

In the Qur'anic chapter of The Cave, Moses encounters al-Khidr as a wise old man by the sea who leads him through a series of trials in which Moses rushes to wrong judgments about al-Khidr's actions. It's a warning against impatience and a parable of humility. Others have found him walking on water, and he's often depicted riding a magical fish. Whatever he is, he dwells immortal at the mouth of rivers as a guide to those in spiritual or physical strife.

I awoke to the sound of chattering and the thick smell of wood smoke and went out to drink tea with the shadows by the fire. Mohammed's brother Mustafa (a small man who looked like Anthony Hopkins, in an oversized brown suit jacket and navy-blue woollen hat) and their teenage neighbour Abdullah (in full football kit and of no known lookalike).

"When I was your age, I walked here from Casablanca," said Mohammed, "I'd walk for fifteen kilometres then sit down wherever I was and watch people go about their lives. Every day I'd think, 'maybe I'll meet my wife in the next village and stay there until I die.' But I never did, and I never married. And here I am."

And there we were. His brow was sullen for a beat as we stared at the flames before bursting into fits of laughter that devolved into rasping coughs. Tales of walking great distances as part and parcel of life are often heard from the older generations: roaming on foot from country to town in search of work or bread (in the case of the Moroccan author Mohamed Choukri). Yet here was a self-declared rambler errant, out and intent for romance. A failed one, yes, but the memory of the intention still flickered mirth across his murky gaze. It was a challenge to my ever-wavering sense of beginnings and endings.

I wondered how he knew the distances and spoke like a member of the Académie. His fluency was even more remarkable in the deafening silence of his brother. The answer was likely a sound memory and plain attention. (And my inferior French.) He responded to such questions with shrugs—the tale was more important than its details. Yet, despite the settling calm, I remained anxious to reach Souiria.

"Be patient. It's not in your hands," Mohammed said again. Time passed, we drank tea, I slept, Mohammed hummed, but the river roared. It never occurred to me to doubt his ability to judge the sea. The tides were written on his face.

The sun eventually disappeared behind our camp in the dunes. I had been adamant about reaching Souiria even though I had nowhere to stay. Loathe to admit it, what I desired was the certainty of a café. For Wi-Fi, for passing fame, rather than tea leaves and fireside spirituality. Though, in the moment, I was restless. Pseudo-poetic and obscure, sure, but restless.

Mohammed, a good fellow by nature and praiseworthy by name, turned to me with a smile that had listened to my thoughts and suggested staying the night with him. "Cross the river in the morning," he said. I merely nodded under eyes heavy with fire.

"The world is a beautiful place," he said, "go anywhere, Brazil, America, Russia, France, and be with people just as you are with me now. The only place you can't sit," he paused for a dramatic rasp, "is on the moon," high-pitched cackle.

"Take care of your soul Jimmy [sic], and your body will take care of itself. Use the solitude of walking to reflect on your life and destiny."

Ah, heck, this was al-Khidr—Green Knight to my Gawain. He lived by the elements, and the elements lived by him, the wise watchman at the mouth of the Tensift.

The village of Zawiyat Sidi Hsayen was a short walk through the dunes. The name pointed to the existence of the spiritual—or at least the spiritually dead ("zawiyat" refers to the presence of a Sufi shrine)—between the sands. I had neither the presence of mind to ask about Sidi Hsayen at the time nor could I find anything about him now. And just as well. Whether Higher Truth or Higher Nonsense, it has taken the passing of several years for the mystical in this encounter to force its way out of the physical. And with no amount of magical fish.

Mohammed and Mustafa's house was a courtyard with a rainwater well, a stable and a room with three mattresses arranged in a semi-circle in front of a TV. Mustafa, who never smiled or spoke to me directly, presented a bucket of water and a bottle of shampoo and motioned to the stable. I sponged myself down in the dark and came out shivering in my boxers to find Mohammed bent over a bucket, arms covered in soap, washing my socks, shirt and trousers.

"They were dirty and smelled," was his explanation as he slopped and foamed.

We ate boiled eggs dipped in salt and laughing cow cheese with bread, washed down with several pots of tea. Mustafa flicked through the channels to an Egyptian film, and I pined for the Cairo sunrise. But before nodding off, I distinctly heard Mohammed say: "Watch out for the people in the next town; they aren't as friendly as us."

5

"Oh, what smooth, smooth spoons I'm going to make for myself when I'm a shepherd!"

Miguel de Cervantes, *Don Quixote*

MOHAMMED ASSURED ME THAT THE BEST time to cross the river would be between 8.30 and 9 am. I took his specificity to be heartening, or at least heartfelt, rather than dubious. His still-refusing-to-talk-to-me-for-some-reason-known-only-to-himself brother, Mustafa, switched on the radio, and we dipped bread in argan oil, and it was full and wholesome. Mohammed sat by the door smoking and nodding to the music, occasionally turning to laugh and check I was watching. When I came to put my shoes on, he shook his head and ducked into a little cupboard. He re-emerged with two insoles newly fashioned from a bit of old tyre.

"That's better," he said, and he tutted too at my attempt to sew up my trousers: "If only we had more time."

I noted their phone numbers and promised to ring if I got into trouble on the other side. Then, back on the beach, my heart sank because the river hadn't.

"Wait an hour," said Mohammed, "drink some tea, and the tide will turn."

I was stuck in a tidal loop. It was 9.30, the sun was already hot and I had a fair old way to trek. Perhaps this was another of al-Khidr's trials, but I was keen to move despite yesterday's fleeting mindfulness. I prepared my bag, slid off my trousers and waded in at a mad dash towards the narrowest point of the flow.

I immediately realised I'd left my stick and cap on the shore. Tarboush is the generic word for a hat in Morocco, which to my more Egyptian ear means "fez." So I was somewhat taken aback to hear Mohammed pronounce from the shore:

"Your fez and your cane, sir!" I turned to find him, trousers off, dashing with my stick and cap into the fastest part of the river.

"Come on, Jimmy, this way!" Mohammed bellowed and stormed headlong into the current. He teetered and was knocked clean off his feet. And in that instant, the folklore wobbled too in the absence of any supernatural salmon. He got up straight away, shaking, took a few steps back to steady himself and faced me, dripping.

"The river's too strong," he said, somewhat resentfully, as he handed over the stick and cap. We shook hands, and I set off again. Mohammed returned to the sand to sit and watch. I, too, fell up to my waist, but after a few heavy strides with my bag above my head, I made the shore. The green man of the Tensift now sat in his baggy y-fronts on the other bank.

Mustafa suddenly appeared without ceremony beside me as I was drying off and getting dressed. He was wearing only a pair of yellow boxer shorts and carrying a plastic bag in one hand. Unabashed as if he was just on his daily commute, and this was his uniform. Crikey. Just as quickly as he appeared, he walked off into town. No glance shared, no word uttered. I looked back, and Mohammed had vanished too. I knew even then that our meeting would be the finest hour. But there must always be hope for more, so I turned my heels for Safi, leaving the ocean to return to the waves.

—

Spells are just as soon lifted as if they had never been. I was lured by the café across from the compact little 16th-century Portuguese castle of Fort Agouz. We glowered at one another's weathered wooden entrances over several espressos, and I fired off a blog post. Spacious and empty was the town. And fulfilled this fool.

Barnacled rocks crunched underfoot, and a cool spray drifted from the waves. I marched along a glorious cliff path overlooking the smooth surf peeling onto jagged rocks below.

It wasn't long before I came upon the first of a series of enormous industrial complexes that would dominate the day. I was shepherded by fences up to the main road with every new factory that erupted out of an otherwise pristine coastline. Several times—strained by tarmac—I scrambled down the cliffs determined to re-join the sea, only to find my path blocked by razor wire, nappies and beer bottles.

Passing traffic would generally turn their heads out of passing interest or stop to see if I was lost. The positive honkers, the negative honkers. Today virtually every car came with an enthusiastic thumbs-up or a bottle of water. I probably only noticed this when my spirits were in the asphalt. Workers waiting for buses applauded and gestured to sore legs. Police officers cheered me through the checkpoints.

The final approach to Safi was along a road lined with fish factories and houses that crumbled into the sea. An energising cocktail of decay that inspired a swift two-step. Groups of men stood under shacks, sipping coffee and watching without expression. But with a wiggle of my stick came blessings of peace and those hardened faces melted into easy smiles neath stern brows.

Darkness fell as I settled at a terrace in the centre of town. Hopelessly expecting replies from Couchsurfing hosts, but none was to be had this night. The waitress cleaned my table four times, each more diligently than before, before I got the message and checked into a hotel across the street with the prospect of a day's rest before my next rabies jab.

—

You can't move for 16th-century Portuguese ramparts along the Atlantic coast of Morocco. You've seen one; you've seen them all. Safi is no exception and boasts Africa's only Gothic cathedral. Built by the Portuguese in 1519, it sits below street level opposite the Grand Mosque, whose 11th-century minaret was destroyed during its construction—How Very Gothic. Safi, or Asfi as it is known locally ("Safi" being the jumbled up, European rendering of the name), is homonymous with a Darija word for "okay"—picture the 16th-century scene:

Portuguese: Olá, old chap! Would you mind awfully if we built a fort here? You see, we're doing a thing all along the coast, and we'd hate to leave a fort-less gap in your lovely little port.

Moroccan: Go away, you colonial ****.

Portuguese: What did you say it was called?

Moroccan: Okay, that's it, you ***** we warned you...

Portuguese: Come again?

Moroccan: Safi, you ****.

Portuguese: Safi?

Moroccan: *******.

Portuguese: Safi! What a lovely name! We'll get started with the fort straight away. Also, I feel a Gothic cathedral, perhaps where that lovely minaret is.

It was presumably to distance itself from such Portuguese and Gothic tendencies that in 1999 Safi entered the Guinness Book of Records by cooking up the world's biggest tajine. In honour of this, I devoured five on the same day.

—

A tall archway at the old fort in Safi stands as a window on the horizon. Point your camera at a certain angle, and you can almost pretend the industrial fishing port to the right is not there.

Two days of scrubbing clothes, scribbling notes and recharging through reading. "I am not one of my country's scholars nor one of its philosophers, but I am a lover of knowledge: knowledge is why I set out on this journey...," claims the protagonist of Naguib Mahfouz's *The Journey of Ibn Fatouma*. And I almost believed it, drifting in the cafés dreamy—the same romantic aromas that had first enticed me to Cairo.

Even *Don Quixote* shares this sentiment, "He who reads and travels sees and learns." This is precisely the thing the lone traveller needs: reassurance that all doubts and fears mean something. It would take a considerable amount of time until I became post-Quixote, whereupon I'd consider such a mindset is just as likely to lead to mental illness (or, at the very least, a skewed perspective on humdrum daily encounters). But it was a fun thought at the time.

Indeed, before setting out on this walk, I had imagined all the smooth spoons I would make as a shepherd. That is to say, all the miles I would walk, all the people I would meet, the words I word write, the ideas I would form. And here I was as a shepherd making those spoons (so to speak). And now, here I am crafting the final, smoothest spoon of them all. (It was at this point the metaphor stretched so thin I had to go and have a lie down for three years before summoning up the wherewithal to finish the darned spoon.)

Whatever, this was my challenge and I was high, that day, on espresso, roasted chicken and errant ego. I spat sonnets from the corners of tiled coffee houses among an assortment of scrunched-up faces—men with leather jackets and no sheds. I munched shortbread smothered in sesame seeds in the covered souqs devoid of tourists. I smouldered at the seagulls slung in the winds over the harbour wall. I revelled in being utterly aimless.

The following morning, one of the nurses at the vaccine clinic looked at my passport, then at me and said, "My God, you're old!" Then came a brief lecture about Gamal Abdel Nasser and the history of Arab nationalism, culminating in two sharp pricks on my shoulder.

Afterwards, the nurse pulled up a map on his phone to calculate the distance to Casablanca, "250 kilometres, blimey," he said and then motioned to my flip-flops with no hint of sarcasm: "buy some shoes."

I'd been the only case of rabies that month, so, in a way, I was pleased to have provided some excitement (the jabs are entirely free). Three nurses, the doctor and the receptionist all stood in a line to shake my hand and wave me off.

—

Walking along the Atlantic coast of Morocco isn't all sunshine and sandy beaches. Mostly it's pavements and pampers. I climbed out of Safi under a determined downpour. Halfway up, a security guard ran over for a high-five: I'd join you if it weren't for this bad foot, he promised, and hopped over a puddle for emphasis.

Further on, I met a shepherd walking toward me through the deluge on the other side of the road. He shouted for me to put my jacket on. I was generally averse to sweating in soaked Gore-Tex but hadn't accounted for the peer pressure of a concerned herdsman. So, reluctantly, I paused under a tree to fix my various coverings if only to please the man who, for reasons known only to him and the goats, had sat on the wall to make sure I did.

Along cliff tops of narrow animal tracks, skipping over grey stones under even greyer skies. Along the shore, lone men stood on rocky outcrops staring out to sea: no fishing lines or livestock in sight. I judged them to be composing lyrical ballads or tinkling in unison to the wind.

Around midday, I came upon a couple of weathered and barefoot men slouched by a wall enjoying a sudden outburst of sun. One gestured with a hand as if patting a dog. "Come over here," it suggested, so I perched on my bag beside them. The man of the invisible dog produced a gnawed and stale disc of bread from a jacket pocket. I said I wasn't hungry. Where have you walked from? Where are you going? But your family? A wife? A job? Why don't you have a bike? I got as far as Ibn Bat- before:

"You're lying," he said, tapping the bread on his knee and gazing into the depths of my folly before continuing, "au revoir monsieur." The second man said as much in Arabic, and I walked off clueless. Was it the bread, the absence of dog, or were they a couple of disenchanted descendants of the great Ibn Bat-?

As I arrived, a blanket of dark clouds was creeping upon the red, blue and grey box houses of the village of Bedouzza. I had reached the tip of a long, narrow S-curve stretching back to Agadir. Flipping the map on its side rendered the remaining way to Tangier all downhill. Let it come down. I considered this a significant enough non-event to warrant an afternoon off.

A rowdy pickup truck was parked outside the white and olive-green lighthouse at cape Bedouzza, a building that looked like a sunken castle reclaimed by the sands. "You just missed the football, mate!" said the truck. Morocco had just defeated Cameroon, and the café opposite was full of the post-match ash and up-turned cups, their fortunes scattered on the tables.

Abdelmajid, the waiter, said he knew someone with a bed for the night. Nature documentaries on the TV, coffee and a box of millefeuille, to the constant put-put of the sebsi surrounds, as I wrote up the day's thoughts of nappies and potholes. Should I ever run for local government, I should like to have it on record that my enjoyment of the pipe was only secondhand. Though, firsthand, it might have helped with the adverbs.

It was almost sunset when Abdelmajid returned with a man called Mustafa, who reeked of the pipe. His red eyes popped as he swayed in a merry trance. He took me at a giggle to a second café and introduced me to a Mohammed, who pointed across the street to the bright blue house of a certain Abdelqader.

I handed Mustafa some coins for his trouble since he otherwise seemed keen to stagger with me to Tangier and knocked on Abdelqader's blue door. "Hello, um, peace, er, Abdelmajid, Mustafa, Mohammed, Ibn Battutah, just passing through, a spare bit of floor etc.?" I think I was more surprised at my stuttering than he was.

"Inshallah," he said before leading me upstairs to a flat that could be mine for a steal at 3,000 dirhams (£250). Citing some holier-than-thou policy of random financial interactions, I walked straight out the door, but we agreed on

100 (£8ish) a few steps later. He would try to return the money later, feeling guilty since, as he admitted, he'd been told a foreign man was wandering around looking to buy a flat. I refused for the same reason.

That evening was spent with Abdelqader's family in and around a pile of roasted sardines and a large red onion. We watched a TV programme called *al-Mustakshifun* (The Explorers).

"Just like you!" said Abdelqader's wife Rabia, and I puffed out my chest for effect. She moulded mashed fish meat into tiny balls, and I chomped on my onion. The conversation remained somewhat stilted but was, nonetheless, aromatic.

"The thing is," said Rabia, "we understand you, but you can't understand us. But don't worry, our daughter will be home soon, and she speaks Egyptian."

We mixed gestures with the odd, often unrelated, word in French. When Iman, the daughter, arrived, she introduced herself in the Syrian dialect. "How's my Egyptian?" she smiled. "It's not," I said. We were stuck at a crossroads of four Arabic vernaculars where words frequently led to different or no meaning.

"I just assumed any Arabic on TV that's not Moroccan was Egyptian," she said, citing hours spent watching Turkish soaps dubbed into Syrian. The Syrian dialect is much closer to Egyptian than Moroccan, so I could finally communicate just how much I was enjoying the onion (crunch crunch).

Ashraf, the son, arrived from football training and Rabia instructed the children to show me their homework. Fair enough, since I'd introduced myself as an English teacher. They rolled off presentations about wavelengths, equations and Morocco's weather ("It's windy along the coast"). They sure knew their onions. All the while, Abdelqadar watched from the sofa, reciting the phrase "Sobhan Allah" (basically: isn't God just smashing!). He smoked endlessly and interrupted his children to tell of past fishing trips from Safi: "One time we hauled in a large net of sardines, and there was lightning, and then a whale crashed into the boat, and I woke up and had been dreaming." Not quite Hemingway, but the ports would be empty if all fishermen did it for the allegory.

Rabia, a hive of activity and giggles from the kitchen where she was now kneading bread, asked about the people I'd met and the Moroccan customs, traditions and foods I'd encountered.

"All the things you must have experienced!" she said, "What a challenge! I want to do that too!"

A discussion ensued between husband and wife: "Let's head down to the beach tomorrow and walk up to the far end and back," "Yes! Yes! Yes!" "How far?" "Ten kilometres?" gasps and exclamations of: "There is no god but God."

It was this word "challenge"—tahhadi—that most Moroccans I'd meet would use rather than my non-committal "journey" or "walk." Uncertain of "adventure" as a manifestation of privilege—the idea of collecting fluff to then write about pebbles. But despite the fact I had barged unannounced into their lives, perhaps I had sparked an idea. Rabia buzzed with energy at the talk of tahhadi.

The general Arabic verb "to walk," in Morocco means merely "to go" after which you must specify how—by donkey, car, or foot. Of course, a similar construction exists in Spanish and French and no doubt many other languages and elsewhere in the Arabic world, but it was only after having the same conversations day in, day out ("where are you going?" / "I'm walking to Tangier" / "walking how?" / "by foot" / "oh") that it struck me as odd and somehow significant. An obvious point, sure, but that didn't stop me, then, from revelling in the bracing brashness of being an English speaker. How bold it is to walk alone without needing a perambulating preposition.

It struck me then, mid-onion (or rather, months later after a conversation with an Iraqi man in a Kensington pub), that the very name of the Moroccan dialect of Arabic, Darija, is cognate with a verb meaning "to walk." The same word is also the root for words like "step," "drawer," "bicycle" (and, bizarrely, the Classical Arabic term for "pheasant"). If anywhere has a language for walking, then it's Morocco.

Etymologists (and my teachers at university) would cry nonsense at such wishful deduction, weeping over their prized Hans Wehr Arabic doorstop dictionaries. Darija, they'd shriek, comes from a later meaning of the root—"to be in circulation," "to be used commonly," that is, the "common tongue." An Algerian friend reminded me that Arab philologists traditionally saw nomads as the preservers of the high language. If this isn't an argument in favour of the wayfaring scholar and the language of walking, then I don't know what is. (I'm not sure what all this has to say about pheasants. Honk, probably.)

But, as Tim Mackintosh-Smith warns, "Semitic etymology is perilous territory: it is a wilderness of meaning haunted by fascinating mirages, and it is easy to make things mean what one wants them to mean." Honk indeed. But boy, I love those mirages.

A news story flashed across the TV: a fatal train crash in Rabat. "Maybe you're right, James," Rabia said, eyes fixed on the screen, "Walking by foot would be safer."

We gorged on oranges and endless amounts of mint tea infused with sage. Stiff and sweet. Like my ankles. Concentration slowly faded as Iman tired of translating, and sleep came in an achievement of allium.

I was on the road before daybreak, armed with a bag of sardine meatballs. Abdelqader kissed me twice on each cheek at the top of a path between two houses and I set off along the rocks. Hundreds of seagulls hung in silhouette as we crossed into the day. They were flocking over a shrine on a rocky promontory, surrounded by breakers and peppered with men fishing in their underwear.

The morning was heavy going over soft sand. I soon tired of the slog and found my way back through the dunes and up the cliff.

After many dreary hours in the hard shoulder, I reached a sharp bend where someone had written "Winner's Corner" on the barrier and there, like a loser, I tumbled down a gorge of thickets and loose stones back to the sea.

I walked between rows of narrow, rectangular fields on the borders of waves and slopes. The fields were brimming with tomatoes the size and shape of swollen knees. Workers looked up from their pickings, waved, and then returned to the soil—things to be done.

I walked for a time with a man who had more teeth than hair. Noticing teeth in foreign lands is a habit that betrays a tendency for over-describing to cover up an otherwise meaningless encounter. You can discover much about someone from their teeth, but only if you know what lettuce says about destiny. With language barriers and desperate attempts to comprehend the slightest hint of a quotable syllable, attention tends to linger on the mouth.

Such details feel essential. Fleshes out the character or enamels it, at least. I haven't the foggiest what this man was doing or why save that he seemed interested in Arsenal and was heading to get a bus and was slightly perturbed that I wasn't.

Fast, painless walking, and it was early afternoon when I crested the final dune to Oualidia and its charmingly cemented caravan parks. Oualidia, I'd been told over the last week, would be the highlight of my entire journey along the Moroccan coast. The stunning beaches, the majestic lagoons. But I arrived via the gated holiday villas and saw-you-coming tourist restaurants. Following my upturned nose, I found a sombre purple café up the hill in the waft of hashish. With my Couchsurfing requests unsuccessful, I ventured to the waiter about kipping there for the night, "Bon voyage monsieur," was his only response.

The same happened at the following few places over one long bitter espresso of an afternoon. I eventually found myself in the purple café, again, unfocussed but staring intently like those around, all stranded for work because of lingering storms. And there's me, mildly inconvenienced that a well-practised gaze (struck somewhere between "I belong here," "I don't care what you think" and "please love me") hadn't inspired life-long friendship.

I took a room in a guesthouse across the road and drank milk from the rooftop in the reflection of the violet glow of the café and the twilight sky. A pair of storks settled into a bulging cacophony atop the minaret opposite. Three months in jail is the penalty for disturbing storks. There is an old Amazigh tale that these lanky birds used to be humans that transformed long ago. Another says that they originated in a particularly naughty imam who once got drunk and fell off a minaret when giving the call to prayer. I lost myself in thoughts of what it meant to be a naughty imam, subsequently got legless on dairy and dozed off to the constant chatter of leaden brows, contemplating prison.

6

"There is nothing so undesirable for the high-minded traveller as the sight of his or her own countrymen and women following their guidebooks along the same path."

Lucy Lethbridge, *Tourists*

FAST WALKING IN THE DARK along the mud at the lagoon's edge. I was attuned to the world's sounds but aware only of my squelching. Nevertheless, I heard the flock of sheep before them me and was able to slip over a wall and clamber up the hill without so much as a claggy bleat. In my excitement, I blundered into a farmhouse and excited the jowls of a chained yapper.

After being scared by the dog into a frenzy of bog, I arrived at the road to find my path blocked by a couple of elderly ladies. They were bent over a bucket, washing clothes. They looked up and stared at my messy state but settled for asking why I had a stick. "I'm old," I said, complete with a twirl, and they laughed and stood up, mechanically.

Then, in an odd moment, we all began hobbling around and pretending we had crocked backs. We laughed at the strangeness of it all for a few minutes—even cursing some distant French bells—before they returned to their suds and let me pass. Hours of tarmac later, I pulled into a shop and asked a young man leaning against the counter the way to the sea.

"Follow that tractor," he said, pointing over my shoulder. I did, and shortly before reaching the beach, he caught up with me. "Monsieur! Monsieur!" he said through gasps, "You know it's much slower to walk on sand than on the road?" Of course I knew. But hey, champ, this is my walk, and I'm sticking with it. Wrong or not. Even a swamp is less painful than a road as unforgiving as the horizon. Well, temporarily at least, but I wasn't going to let on.

Mustafa had been on his way to work but saw me as a better offer. We walked on, or rather waded through, a few hours of sand. One long and lively sink before we gave up and found our way through a network of muddy pools back to the road. Mustafa spoke excitedly about what I was doing, expounding on the sheer tahhadi— challenge. "If only I'd met you earlier in the year," he said, "I didn't have a job then and could've walked to Tangier." What to me so often felt overwhelming to him became the liberation of a physical test and the sheer joy of not having to work.

"When you reach Sidi Abed," he said, "ask for Ahmed's café and show him my photo. He'll find you somewhere to sleep."

We took a selfie then Mustafa hurried off to the fields where he should have been picking tomatoes. I cursed every second of tarmac, though rarely was I the only walker on these roads. All shared them: shepherds, school kids and commuters with no recourse to car, cart or cycle. All together in the slow ways of function.

Paths that go against the more leisurely tradition of western-style hiking routes that start from nowhere, pass through nowhere, and end up in the middle of a different nowhere. These are the old ways in the natural flow of the land that start from your front door and, if you're lucky, end up everywhere.

After ten hours and over 50 kilometres of drizzle and the weary scepticism of petrol station kiosks, I shuffled into Sidi Abed along with a train of children returning from school. I entered the first café and asked the waiter for Ahmed. He stared at me and the picture of

Mustafa. "He looks nice," he said eventually, before adding, "there's no one called Ahmed here."

"But you can sleep in the café, no problem," he continued and walked off as if I'd just asked him the time of day. The place was full of shore-ridden fishermen. Cursing the rough seas, bent low over small cups and puffing on their sebsis. I sat at a free seat and finished my bread and cheese under a canvas roof buffeting wildly in the gale. Huddles of men watching football, the pipes a-popping while boys played marbles in the neon of the terrace.

It had been the longest day of the trip so far, and I was simply content to be damp and ignored. I stuffed my priciest items into my pockets and was just settling down to some shut-eye, arms through my bag in a dead man's hold, when the man at the next table leaned over:

"You aren't from round here, are you?"

I launched into my spiel and could tell from his smile that I'd had him at "Ibn." The crowded caps all turned to watch this son of a son of a duck. It wasn't long before he, Lutfi, offered me a meal and a bed at his house in the village up the hill. He rang his wife and told her to put a few more potatoes in the tajine. I clambered on his motorbike and hung on tight, stick resting over the handlebars and bag hanging off the back as we raced up the hill through a labyrinth of pot-holed lanes. Lutfi—whose name in Arabic has the root meaning of "kindness"—is married to Latifa, of the same root. Their five-year-old daughter, Kanza ("treasure"), shook my hand and, their one-year-old, Sukayna ("calm"), proffered a fuzzy cheek.

Latifa heated a pot of water for me to wash away the day, which I did, starkers in the courtyard. Then we sat down to a chicken tajine in a little room full of mattresses, followed by tea, grapes, walnuts and bananas. In the aftermath, Latifa sat breastfeeding Sukayna in the corner, and Lutfi talked about village life.

"Most people here are illiterate; the school is far away, and there aren't enough buses," he said, "Luckily, you found me; I get the idea of exploring somewhere new."

Lutfi was an electrician and had built the family home, managed by Latifa, who was from the northern Rif mountains. They spoke together in a dialect of Tamazight and Darija, but Lutfi's speech to me was tempered with High Arabic and Even Higher Hashish. It was the rhythm of my twenties and rendered the whole affair slightly less translucent, though his eyes shone bright enough.

"We live right next to the largest industrial complex in Africa but get nothing from it."

When Latifa took the children to bed, Lutfi snuck his hand under the television set, pulled out a small, dark green square wrapped in Clingfilm, and set about refilling his sebsi.

"The eighties were the best years," he said as he sat back in the growing cloud, "if you had a dream then, you could achieve it."

I asked him what his dream had been:

"To be an electrician and to build my own house."

Like him, the perfection of the moment was soon lost to a different plane. I fell asleep content in the hearth of kindnesses, treasure and calm under the homely patter of rain on tiles.

The roof was still a-drip at dawn, and the air was awash with baked bread, pancakes, mint tea and frying butter. We sat among the mattresses—dip, eat, sip—in the comfort of silence shared after a heavy storm. Lutfi dropped me back at Sidi Abed, and I was on my way carrying a large bag of walnuts as Latifa's gift.

The route to El Jadida cut through the immense Jorf Lasfar phosphorus plants, a prospect that was every bit as emetic as a travel blog is embarrassing. Grey and beige vistas in a bitter and acidic air. At one point, I stepped in a puddle of foul-smelling, white sludge, which was the highlight of the day.

Passing under a bridge in my slime-covered shoes, I strode through the broken glass of the verge to be intercepted by a lanky boy who came from the side and trailed me, demanding money. I ignored this for as long as I could before turning to face him, "What's your name? How old are you? Where are you going?" I said, in an opening barrage calculated to bamboozle. And to my surprise, he answered in order: "Wa'i, 17, home, then going swimming."

And just as he'd appeared, he disappeared into a field, but not before shouting over his shoulder: "Come and eat at my house." Despite the opportunist begging, his intentions may well have been honest, but the landscape had dulled my nerves, so I bit my lip and walked on.

It was a stream of endless trucks and piles of rocks and rubbish among the general drabness of industry into El Jadida. When the Portuguese were forced out of Morocco in 1769 (cheers and applause), they destroyed what they could, and the remains of this town became known as El Mahdouma—"The Ruined." On its rebuilding, it was named El Jadida—"The New."

I took the left fork at a crossroads where a lighthouse skulks between a cemetery and a petrol station. Once again, slipping seamlessly from the empty spaces between towns to become yet another face in another background. However, both are to stand out, what with a lump of a bag and a perpetual stink.

I took shelter from a sudden downpour in a café near the 16th-century Portuguese (yawn) church. I found security in an espresso amongst the general herbalities of a Moroccan afternoon while studiously ignoring another European type, similarly ensconced in Gore-Tex at the back. Presumably, we were both intent on being the only intrepid traveller in these parts. My host for that night, Bessar, and her partner pulled up after a while to save the foreigners and their egos.

They told me of El Jadida's fame as they drove: its fish, lighthouse and Portuguese ramparts. The big three of Moroccan towns on the Atlantic coast. Nothing novel, despite the town's name. Their flat in the outskirts overlooked a square of artificial grass, and with incredible kindness and trust, they handed over the keys for two nights; if the neighbours ask, I'm to say I'm a distant cousin.

To make something of the evening, I went across the square to the mahlaba (that ubiquitous Moroccan dairy institution) for a boiled egg sandwich and a glass of milk. A patchwork dog watched from the floodlit football pitch, scratching a troublesome ear as I chewed in silence, contemplating a day of rest.

—

The dog was still there early the following day, scratching the other ear, as I lazed over a spread of white harira (a thick and bracing breakfast soup made from semolina, milk and topped with olive oil (also called belboula)). I lounged on the terrace corner for half the morning, off-duty and carefree in flip-flops with my essentials in a canvas bag. Around me, men read the papers propped on wooden sticks or scrolled the socials on sagging necks.

After breakfast, I flipped my feet to the wind and flopped down to the long sands jam-packed with football games. I watched for a time as a woman in a niqab chased about with the men, her face fully covered but her knees and bare elbows flapping in the breeze.

The cobbled lanes of the old town were bursting with pregnant cats and American tourists. Outside the Church of the Assumption, I listened to a tour guide explain that "Morocco has four seasons during the year and is great friends with Donald Trump." I assumed he was about to launch into some surreal free verse, so I snuck off before I got a headache.

I dozed for the rest of the afternoon on the esplanade, slumped on a chair between Bessar and her friend Mohsin. I drifted in and out of their diatribe against the state of education and talk of a group of Moroccan adventurers who'd recently crossed Africa by skateboard. I was learning that it's often better to travel in silence, to listen to the follies of others so you may, for a moment, forget your own. Showing enthusiasm to some often inspires them to diminish it in the face of their great aunt's cleaner's nephew who once pogo-sticked to the South Pole—"now that's a proper adventure," and all agree with knowing and pitiful glances. Later that evening, in a dingy bar reminiscent of the town's ruined past, another friend of Bessar's, Yacine, eyed me over a cigarette:

"You have a green bag, right?"

He took an exaggeratedly long draw on his cigarette that told me lung cancer would be preferable to listening to another European who thinks he's doing something remarkable. I knew my place, and it was in bed under a heavy blanket, agitated and scratching, like the dog of my morning.

Once a year, Morocco invites the best Saudi horses to a state-of-the-art equestrian centre just outside El Jadida. Today was the finale of this year's do, and the roads were lined with flags and bored police, so my half-day tramp to the next town, Azemmour, was in the ditch of a dual carriageway. Doing my bit to protect Saudi gee-gees from dangers in the peripheries.

Portuguese explorer Ferdinand Magellan is said to have sustained a severe knee wound after losing his horse in battle near Azemmour in 1513. The injury forced him to walk with a limp for the rest of his days.

I arrived at Café Atlantis in Azemmour mid-morning, knee over knee and very much sans cheval. I had much time to pass before my host for the night, Zakaria, was due to appear. And pass it did, slowly, while silently bristling at the group of loud, artsy youths (read: had twirly moustaches) behind me. Eventually, several hours and multiple, increasingly existential emails with Zakaria later ("I'm here," "I am also here," "But surely we can't *both* be here?"), the youth with the curliest tips came over and introduced himself as Zakaria.

"What do you wanna do?" he asked as we walked back to his flat to dump my bag. His digs were a temporary affair in a dusty neighbourhood of box apartment blocks and skips that merged with the surrounding dust. It was all strings, cushions and old tajine pots—a student's home, he told me, for days spent drinking espresso and playing Spanish guitar by the river. So this is what we did.

In the 16th century, a slave from Azemmour called Mustafa Azemmouri, an expert in natural medicine (and so, by contemporary standards, a wizard), was taken by Christopher Columbus as the ship's doctor for his voyage to America. At least such was the version recounted to me by Zakaria. I've since found no corroborating evidence. The most established legend of this Mustafa (or Estevanico, "Little Stephen") is that he was enslaved to a Spaniard, was the first known African to arrive in America, and would go on to become the first black explorer of the American south. A magical tale in its own right. I wouldn't cross paths with Big Chris until Seville in Spain, and even then, he was dubious (the tomb is rumoured to contain his brother) and dead.

This town, named after a wild olive tree, presents one long trunk of tarmac bursting with cafés (all named after either the town, the sea, or the river (apart from Café Aloha, because #variety)). The road eventually bumps into the Portuguese ramparts and fans up a hill in a network of souqs to the shrine of a Sufi sheikh before sloping down again to a Jewish shrine by the river.

We ate a mound of couscous and then climbed the ramparts where Zakaria strummed flamenco as a football match played out below on flagstones emblazoned with dragons, the emblem of this enchanting town. I slept against the bricks in the warmth of simple company and a life of simple purpose.

I was quite enamoured by Azemmour—enazemmoured, if you will. The corniche splashed in vibrant colours and bedragonned stones, and the couples floating in wooden boats, spinning in the eddies of Oum Er-Rbia.

The river banks were bordered by the sheer and precarious architecture of the old town, itself crammed full of crumbling buildings and fading graffiti from when a festival of artists once laid wonder to its walls.

"There's nothing to do in Azemmour apart from sitting in the cafés and drinking coffee," said Zakaria as we sat in a café drinking coffee. And I was beginning to understand that there is a refined art in the slow taste of quick coffee. I wondered how coffee houses were once such hives of intellectual activity that they'd turn into insurance firms at the slightest provocation.

We sipped and sipped, and Zakaria eulogised on cannabis (of which Morocco is the world's largest (illicit) producer). Gather some friends and a tent, he said, and head off into the heart of the Rif mountains. That's Moroccan tripping.

Five months later, somewhere in the forest of Brocéliande, Brittany, I met a jittery man called Guillaume who'd spent a few months roaming the Rif. He'd tramp along, he told me, with a red guitar strapped to his front and a feathered cap on his head. Arriving at each village, he'd produce a magnifying glass and begin setting fire to pine cones, much to the children's amazement. "I became a local legend," he insisted.

"But one day," continued Guillaume, "a kid screamed at me: 'Devil! Devil!' The kid pointed, and all the men came running from the town, throwing stones. I was only saved by the village imam who took me into his home where I fell in love with his blue-eyed daughter."

I'd stumbled across Guillaume in the woods, trembling over a bong near the tomb of the wizard Merlin. Over a bizarre and stilted evening, I learnt that he'd come to this centre of Arthurian legend several years before with a dog, a saxophone and a girlfriend. The girlfriend left the next day to become an actress in Paris.

"I'm sorry," he said, cradling both saxophone and dog as we parted the following morning, "cannabis seems to have affected my social skills." And I think of him now as the fallen troubadour in reflection of Zakaria, the rising minstrel.

"The only problem is that the bloody king controls all the cannabis," said Zakaria. Mohammed VI has more personal wealth than Queen Elizabeth II (he ranks 5th in the world,

Her Maj is 12th). In 2011, the king was modest enough to officially give up his claim of divine appointment. Now he's a mere mortal, albeit one who favours Swiss watches over addressing the 35 million Moroccans living at or below the poverty line. There's no accounting for taste. Literally. It's far easier to maintain a shiny army than to feed the poor, as Tim Mackintosh-Smith has remarked of eternal leaders across the Arabic world.

Appearance is everything. And the monarch remains, in the Western imagination, like his father Hassan II, *Notre ami le roi* (our friend, the king), so reads the title of a book that attacks the pervading view of Morocco as an Islamic country that's more "like us" (that is, like France). All that run-of-the-mill corruption and torture of political prisoners. "Every head of state has its secret gardens," Hassan II once said, letting slip the truth that from city offices to authoritarian regimes, success often depends on subduing the masses through pot plants.

Studying law, living atheism and breathing music is a combination that makes life in Morocco intolerable for Zakaria. When the final exam is done, he vows to step out the door and walk to South Africa with nothing but his guitar. Laurie Lee, like.

I was just passing through—a different town, village or wilderness each day—so any insights into real Morocco would only ever be incidental. Plus, I was conscious that in the general day-to-day of walking, without a regimen of blogs, all I'd remember would be a string of sunsets and desperately needing the loo. So, now at least, I'm grateful for the late nights spent tapping away at a derivative dictionary of the days. It was tired writing, hurried and wary of adjectives, with often only a string of abstract nouns for safety, but it was something. And now it's this.

Another picturesque sky threatened to pierce the clouds as we returned over the hill in dire need of plumbing. Through markets of plastic toys and spice pyramids, picking up meat and vegetables for dinner. Old ladies squatting in doorways propositioned us as we went. "Tikri?" they'd say, "Wanna rent?"

Zakaria laughed, and the women laughed louder. I didn't catch on until one woman suddenly lunged and grabbed my hand, I turned, and she winked and crumpled up her face in a manner I was presumably supposed to find alluring. I shriek-laughed my way out of her grasp and hurried on after the boys with my tail between my legs. Back at the flat, I was suddenly overcome with tiredness (and, who knows, repressed emotion released by the tikri women) and crashed out on the sofa, not to wake until morning.

Zakaria waved me off before sunrise from under a heap of blankets. They'd tried in vain to rouse me for the tajine supper. But I'd been lost in a secondhand cannabis dream where Portuguese horses rented knees from disreputable doorsteps to gallop away from anyone so audacious as to follow a guidebook along the same path as me.

7

تَبَهْلَسَ

Tabahlasa

"To come suddenly from a country without any luggage."

I WAS OFF TO RABAT to meet my sister who'd arrived from London for a cookery class. Unaccustomed ankles and mischievous dogs had scuppered my original schedule and left me five days' short of the capital. So bus it was. Lizzie and I spent several days roaming carefree about the blues and whites of the kasbah. We drank tea among the fat cats of the Andalusian Gardens, gazed across the river mouth to the old pirate republic of Salé (which is more cemetery than corsair nowadays), drew waves and question marks on our arms, did cartwheels at the landmarks and sang on the bridges.

I introduced Lizzie to my daily staples of chickpea soup and staring from café terraces. And she reminded me there was a life full of glitter and disco outside a solo jaunt. Possible futures beckoned and glimmered over games of cards and bottles of wine. It was an abrupt but welcome interruption to the journey. And it was about to get far more abrupt, for I had a wedding to attend.

To explain: my best friend Duncan proposed to his girlfriend the very same week I conceived of walking home to England. Wonderful, joyous, life-affirming, etc. He then asked me to be his best man. Wonderful, joyful, life-affirming, etc., oh-shit-will-have-to-make-a-speech-better-decline-citing-some-holier-than-thou-principle-of-adventure. I eventually came to my senses: life goes on, what the hell, and I had the means. Plus, I wasn't going to miss the once-in-a-lifetime opportunity to spit some rimes of the vagrant wand'rer to a room full of stunned wedding guests.

So it was that, over the past weeks, I had been putting together a rambling rhyme on the move. (Hence my propensity to slip into nonsense verse in the earlier chapters. Apologies.) I'd laid my heart bare to the seagulls, muttered sweet nothings from the terraces, and bored my sister to death with multiple drafts.

The wedding was as weddings are. Full of love and life, friendship and family. There was laughter. There was pizza, cake, comfy sofas, and reality survival shows on TV, and, and.... But before I could get too carried away with home comforts during those two bitterly cold Autumn days in Watford, I was on a plane back to Rabat for my final rabies jab.

I would spend the next week waiting for my bag to join me, however, after it took an unscheduled stop in Madrid. Ample time, therefore, to contemplate the pointlessness of it all deep in the darker reaches of the more obscure dictionaries, where such verbs as the above "tabahlasa" exist for the empty-handed pleasure of the stranded connoisseur. Time enough to consider what this says about the forgetfulness of ancient Arabs and whether this was a bad sign for my bag. As the emptiness dragged on, all I could do was compare my stuttering, nascent life of adventure with the beginning of Duncan and Stephanie's life-long adventure (well, eternal because they are Mormons. But still, yikes).

God, it was stark. But it was also incredibly selfish to wallow in my friends' happiness, so I ate biscuits and read detective stories. "I sometimes wish I'd taken a gentle little job in the Egyptian Civil Service, Lewis," said Inspector Morse in my current Colin Dexter novel. Ah, Egypt, I thought, why had I left? Yes, that's right, the dust, the pollution, the lack of space to properly exercise beyond the confines of a gym without being accosted by taxi drivers, dogs and other pedlars asking for the time of day. But what of those old, high-ceilinged flats with wooden floorboards? What of walking along the Nile by the light of the full moon? What of mango juice? What of...what of...Shoroq? That old flame was long gone. Done and dusted. As Cairo itself. And just like that, my thoughts hovered between worthlessness and hollowness; all that awaited me was a winter without luggage.

It was a week of afternoons at the airport over digestive biscuits and plastic coffee. In the mornings, I busied myself by walking along Rabat's tramlines, dodging rain over espressos and failing to find anything other than boozy Oxford crime thrillers to read. At the cosy, so-called English Bookshop, I picked up *The Question of Writing Poetry of Morocco in English*, to which the answer—after a cursory flick—seemed, without further explanation, to be to write about babies in bathtubs. Instead, and perhaps over-dramatically, I read *Robinson Crusoe*.

Before washing up on the island, Crusoe is enslaved to a pirate for two years in Salé. When

Daniel Defoe was writing, Salé was an enclave of pirates and the seat of the fearsome Barbarossa. After 28 years, (#SpoilerAlert) Crusoe escapes the island and returns to England, crossing the Pyrenees in midwinter, where half of his party is eaten by wolves. And here I was, 28 years old (I'd had a birthday since Chapter One, thank you), on a walk that would, at some point, span all of Salé, the Pyrenees and England. Henceforth, Crusoe became my benchmark for "hey, what's the worst that can happen?"

Today the pirates have all but disappeared (my host, Salman, swore that Salé remains the dodgiest place in Morocco, and a lone wooden corsair (now restaurant and bar) floats on the river below the kasbah). I insist on the acute accent to distance from the English spelling of the place, Sale, which in French means "dirty," which Salé nevertheless is, acutely so. I'd cross the Pyrenees and their wolves in time. For now, there was nothing to do but pick crumbs and remain grateful that I was not enslaved to a pirate.

My bag turned up on Halloween, and I celebrated with a beer and another Inspector Morse novel, reading into the night as the streets flowed under an endless downpour. Salman left for a party at the American Embassy dressed as a doctor—not a frightening one with a gown covered in gore, and all, just a regular physician, which was altogether more disturbing. He returned at midnight, absentmindedly tipped out some sweets from his scrubs and retired to his room without a word—only the rain and the wind for company, with crossword murders and increasingly empty bottles.

"Walk tall, kick ass, learn to speak Arabic, love music and never forget you come from a long line of truth seekers, lovers and warriors," said Hunter S Thompson, presumably of Zakaria and my return for more Cheer and Loafing in Azemmour.

The morning after Halloween, I sat in a café across from the bus station, waiting for a ride back to Azemmour. Over a breakfast of croissants, orange juice and coffee, I watched two policemen smoking under a sign that read "no smoking." Cigarettes exhausted, they began polishing each other's pistols. Hey, where's risk but in a friendly disregard for the rules? In some sense, both acts were the same, I thought, before realising I'd probably been staring at the men for too long. Then, in an ingenious double take (proof I was now back in the Moroccan game), I remembered there is no such thing as staring for too long at a café. A short while later, and in celebration of my newfound wisdom, I missed the bus.

No problem, though, as it took thirty minutes to leave the station (it first had to shake off all the sandwich sellers and other hawkers). So by the time I had bought my ticket, gone to the loo, faffed about for small change to pay for going to the loo, and argued with the man guarding the loo that just because I'm foreign doesn't mean I should pay more than everyone else for doing a piss, and sprinted to three wrong platforms, I was able to simply stroll onto the bus behind a man selling peanuts who'd been beside me at the urinal. Suffice it to say I didn't buy any peanuts for the road.

Back in Azemmour, a new traveller was staying with Zakaria, a Swiss social worker called Sabrina who'd spent the previous summer walking the pilgrimage routes of Europe. Ashamedly, this was the first I'd heard of such things. We ate beef tajine (I remained awake this time). I learnt of a "Camino" and its fabled "de Santiago," then instantly felt guilty that I hadn't known about it before. So, naturally, I didn't check it out again until I was adrift somewhere in southern Spain looking for

Any Bloody Route North and yellow arrows began to appear on lamp posts with such increasing frequency that I began to think it was a sign. Which, to be fair, it was.

That night we drank coffee under the stars as Zakaria played the blues and various kinds of smoke filled the air. There, in that moment, I was delighted to be back, and my own blues slowly began to fade with the prospect of being on the move again. Mustafa, the half-Syrian waiter, wafted in and out now with cigarettes now with warbled ballads from the Levant. All much amused in the spontaneity of song under a sky of shooting stars.

To mark this day, the first of November, I instructed a barber to fix me a moustache. In the Moroccan dialect, getting a haircut is to literally say, "I want to improve myself." So I put myself at the hands of the improver (the barber) and emerged so goddam improved that I've kept the look till this day (2021, that is).

Started by daylight next morning, light and airy, gulping down a bowl of white harira opposite the ramparts. I restocked with dates, crossed the bridge over the river, and was on my way to Sidi Rahal. I improvised a path through the luscious green farmland beyond Azemmour back to the sea. Once more reacquainted with the wide-smiled confusion of the Moroccan countryside. (And just the one teenage boy on a moped demanding money—but it was early, so I had energy enough to humour him until he got bored and whizzed off.) Two men selling fruit and veg by the roadside asked where I was headed. On hearing "Tangier," one shook my hand and said I would never make it and the other kissed my forehead and said a prayer, which I took as a similar vote of confidence.

After 12 hours of solid rain and over 50 kilometres walked, I collapsed, drenched and knackered, at a café by the dunes at Sidi Rahal. The sky, like the town and the faces of the street, was dismal. My phone pinged with a message from the night's host, Zain. "Sorry," he wrote, "but I'm ill and can no longer take you in." I was fuming, and it was no wonder nobody smiled. I attempted my charm at several cafés and was met only with confusion. A lady at an Italian restaurant offered me a villa for the night at 400 dirhams (around £32.)

Of course, this was all relative and no doubt reasonable in other circumstances. It was just me being a charmless and cynical walker. And off to the next café, a dark, low room with blue strip lights and groups of men puffing shisha in the corners. It was dull, heavy and lifeless. I slumped in a corner of my own, and when the waitress came over, I asked her if she knew of any place to stay the night. I watched her go from corner to corner. Eyes glared at me through the gloom. Then she returned.

"No luck!" she said, "But you could always get a taxi to Casablanca; they have hotels there."

I kicked my bag, breaking the last of my digestives. The waitress shrugged and walked off. I slunk deeper into my corner, hidden by the smoke and resigned to a night in the dunes after closing time. I'd long fallen asleep when my phone suddenly sprung to life with another message from Zain.

"Where are you?"

I told him and looked at my watch. It was 11 pm.

"Stay there. I'm coming, be outside in ten minutes."

In my dazed state, I was just about to mount a rather pathetic insistence that he shouldn't go to any trouble, but he had already hung up. Ten minutes later, a black Range Rover pulled up outside, and a man wearing three hooded coats poked a bald head out the window:

"Put your bag in the boot and hop in."

There was no hint of a smile. Dispensing with pleasantries, Zain launched into berating me for not having given an exact arrival time the day before. I explained that that was the thing about walking. At best, I could only provide a two-hour window, which is what I'd done. He fell silent and looked me in the eyes via the rear-view mirror:

"You know what, I'll forgive you," he said, "You have a kind face, and I like your moustache. It's my type."

The man in the passenger seat chose that moment to turn around and introduce himself: Abdelrahman from Holland, the boyfriend, and, as had just become apparent, we shared the same moustache. Apropos of nothing, Zain went on to explain that he had an immune system deficiency and, in the same breath, apologised for not having shaved that morning.

Their house was a four-floor luxury villa. We sat on sofas in the basement, and Abdelrahman brought us harira followed by coffee and date biscuits.

"What are your hobbies?" asked Zain, now lying on his front, watching me with his head propped in his hands.

"Walking," I replied, "Yours?"

"Sex and dancing."

I focussed intently on my soup and turned to Abdelrahman. Originally a baker called Janus from Amsterdam, Abdelrahman had met Zain twenty years ago, fell in love and converted to Islam. Zain insisted that his wife and children in Casablanca are blissfully unaware of his double life. He eventually got bored listening to us talking in English and interrupted in Arabic:

"Ma 'andaksh mushkila law nimt ma'k fi-nefs el-bayt?" (Which I understood to mean "You don't mind me sleeping with you in the same house?")

"Of course not!" tired as I was, I completely missed the strangeness of the question. Zain's eyes widened, and Abdelrahman bade us both a good night, again odd, and Zain beckoned for me to follow him up the stairs. Once in the room and with the door closed, the dirham finally dropped.

"Er Zain, what's going on? Where am I sleeping?"

"With me!"

"Ah."

"The same *bayt*!"

"Hmm."

I promptly learned that the word "bayt" (which in other Arabic dialects means "house/home") in Morocco can mean "bedroom." I apologised profusely for not being gay and was overcome with the awkwardness of apparently offending his hospitality. He flashed his puppy eyes again before retreating to the boyfriend in the basement. I closed the door, got into bed and fell asleep in much the same way that insomniacs don't, my ears firmly trained on the handle.

Zain marched into my room at 7.30 am and told me to come downstairs.

"First, we drink coffee with dates and watch National Geographic for an hour. Then we eat breakfast."

The atmosphere was incredibly cordial, considering what had almost occurred last night. Abdelrahman handed me a cup and saucer with three dates, and we sat in silence, watching a family of gazelles being torn to pieces by a cheetah.

"As the Prophet Muhammad (peace be upon him) said: dates are only good for you when eaten in odd number amounts," said Zain, wearing a grey bandana and matching grey tracksuits today.

"You know James, there are some Moroccans who only use Couchsurfing to have sex with Europeans."

"You-, wha-, are you fu-," I began, before settling for, "Why do you use Couchsurfing then?"

"To have sex with Europeans."

Silence resumed, and another gazelle was mauled to bits on the TV. I apologised, yet again, for not being gay and, changing the subject, spoke of my fascination with Azemmour. Zain was similarly in love with the ancient town, but for a different reason:

"It's where everyone goes for cheap sex."

Now I was desperate to get moving. Searching for an out, I threw in some choice adjectives about ramparts and rivers and even mentioned Zakaria and his troupe of atheist musicians.

"There are no atheists in Morocco, only gay people," said Zain, with triumphant finality.

I gave up and stared at the wall. After further tea, the eventual satiation of the cheetah and (importantly) just one more date, Zain and Abdelrahman finally took the increasingly lengthy silences to be a sign that things had run their natural course, and I was able to say a hasty farewell and get back on the road. I was incredibly grateful for their unquestioning generosity and openness but relieved to be on the move again, however uneven I felt in both mind and dates.

—

Film buffs will tell you that *Casablanca* was set in Tangier and only given the name "Casablanca" because it had a better ring. That and because the film *Algiers* was released only a few years earlier and it was feared that your simple cinemagoer might confuse the one for the other. Fiction and fact are blurred in these parts, so I've written the below in acrostic to avoid further panic.

Coursing away the night on empty beaches through urban bays from surf shops to wine cellars, we rounded Cape Tamaris's headland to meet the Hassan II Mosque, its minaret glistening over twenty kilometres away. At more than 200 metres, it stands beacon-like as Pharos, a wonder of the ancient world. I entered Casablanca through the merchants' entrance—

on a concrete ledge above rocks strewn with plastic—skirting the biggest shopping centre in Africa.

A short distance out to sea lies a shrine to the Sufi saint Sidi Abderrahmane. A tiny rocky islet at the end of an arched bridge where witches tell fortunes and curses are cast out with the seventh wave. Pilgrims come to be healed of infertility or heartache before heading from Morocco mystical to Morocco Mall. Liminal places are shorelines.

Searing foot pain blocked any conscious need for enchantment. I shuffled along the terraces and facilities of the corniche to reach the minaret by sunset. A street cleaner lay fast asleep on the grass, his feet on his broom, and I slept beside him with my feet on my bag.

After several false starts across several false cafés, my host, Ali, and I bumped into each other, somewhat by accident, beside a row of taxis. We took one to his flat in Casablanca's industrial suburb of Ain Saba'. An electrical engineer from the north of Morocco, Ali was quietly spoken but keenly interested (though not so much in Casablanca), telling me: "There's nothing here apart from the corniche and the mosque." Tick, tick.

Between coffee and croissant, we made a morning of it at Ali's local, Café le Point. Large windows and ornate wooden walls decorated with paintings of horses and robed men charging at unseen horrors beyond the frames.

Languorous we in the dark by the frames. But Ali effused enthusiasm and was, for want of a better word (and which probably betrays my latent homesickness), cuddly. He works at the central train station. "My dream job," he said. A dream that grew from a child's obsession with model trains. And he was living out that long curiosity of childhood in his scuffed Dr Martens and black corduroys and with a permanent dazed smile that suggested a half-remembered joke (or, more likely, a full recollection of the choo-choo's of yesteryear).

Ali left me sipping the bitters for a few more hours to write up my journal and consider what Le Point of it all was.

Nap time back at the flat where Ali had just qualified for the football World Cup final by way of FIFA, PlayStation. I woke several hours later to the groans of him losing, and we went out searching for consolation by way of food, stomach. The traditional dish in Casablanca is rfissa—a tajine of lentils, chicken and m'semen (a square, flaky pancake). However, this is usually eaten on Wednesdays, which today wasn't, so we ate chicken and chips instead (works for any day) and took a bus down to the old medina.

Crowded alleys under towering, whitewashed art deco. At the port end sits Rick's Café, that legendary best gin joint in town. A sign on the door says anyone wishing to enter must be dressed in "business casual." The doorman shook his head at my trainers and Ali's cords and docs with an air of "here's looking at you, scumbags." Dreams of finding love in a Casablanca bar all shattered, Ali and I settled for another sunset over the biggest mosque in Africa in a heady mix of apathy at dusk.

A different street cleaner was sleeping on my patch of grass today. We strolled past, along the corniche, and stopped at a hole-in-the-wall joint selling shefenj—like a plain doughnut. It was a stand-up scoff at tiny tables, elbows in your neighbour's dough, kind of affair. The proper Casablanca way to end the day, served with a glass of tea so sickly it was probably brewed by and with doughnuts. The combination was so powerful that it had a similar effect to booze, and Ali and I walked for hours back to the outskirts high on sugar and life and everything (but mostly sugar). Take that, Rick, I slurred as

I crashed out on a mismatch of mattresses and kicked my informal heels for ~~Kansas~~ ~~Algiers~~ ~~Tangier~~ Chapter Eight.

8

"Everyone is always leaving tomorrow."

Paul Bowles talking to Paul Theroux (who left the next day)

ALI AND I LEFT THE FLAT in the dark. We stood for a moment in the pale, broken glow of a flickering street lamp, exchanged promises to meet again for future doughnuts, then parted our separate ways. Him for the trains and me for the trails beyond Café le Point. (After first shovelling down a spread of freshly squeezed orange juice, bread, cheese, croissant and coffee, all for a measly £1.10.) A biting wind blew under a sky that hung heavy and grey. I turned up my collar and followed the rush hour to the beach. There, by the shore, a she-dog was playing with her pups, and my heart melted. All my residual angst disappeared at the sight of that maternal love for a brief moment. Then the bitch suddenly rushed me, and I was forced to spring headlong into the day along the sands towards Mohammedia, my stick flailing behind in growls of lessons not yet learned.

It started to rain, and the rain quickly became incessant. The way along the beach was soon shut, and it was kept by the grand Samir oil refinery (the biggest in Morocco, don't you know). I veered right through a tumbledown of houses and skips to reach the road where a bus immediately emptied an entire ocean of asphalt surface muck into my face. I caught a brief glimpse of the driver's amusement in the mirror, though there was no significant change in my appearance.

It was a grand squelch of a morning to arrive at a café opposite the kasbah in Mohammedia, where the waiter greeted me with a wad of napkins and, wonderfully, shook my hand. It was only 11 am, and I had until 8 pm when Zaki, my host for the night, would finish work. So I settled in for the long drip—draped my coverings over several chairs, wrung out my socks and slowly began to remain sodden and cold. I put on fresh socks and ate some chicken. A ginger cat and her kittens rolled around my feet, oblivious to the damp. I passed the day, tajine by sip, across most of the kasbah's cafés— just another lone man, hood up, staring at the other side of the clouds. At one point, the rain stopped, and I went to the beach to battle with another angry dog and then it rained again.

Mohammedia, "The City of Flowers and Sport," was once called Fedala (a shortened version of the Arabic for "Favour of God") before being renamed in honour of both King Mohammed V and the new refinery. And, as if the town needed more excitement, it was invaded by America in 1942. The troops marched south to Casablanca, ousted the Vichy French and then celebrated with gin at Rick's, all dressed in business casual, naturally. Yes, yes, I know Rick's is fictional. But then, so is the logic of business bloody casual. (Totally fine about it, though, cool, cool, cool.)

If I hadn't been so numb with cold and desperate for the loo, I would've pined for the seaside summers of yore when adventure was in the books (and no one needed the loo). I sat under the awning of Nice View Café and watched the long harbour wall and the grim metallic peaks of the refinery.

What with the presumptuously named café and the odd sensation that I could've been in a seaside town in Devon (sans oil rig), it felt like I'd slipped in time. A jarring yet exhilarating sensation of nostalgia, like reading an English fantasy of midwinter and magic during the height of summer. Plus, I was still suffering from residual fits of nonsense verse. I didn't much thaw and I didn't much thee; the day was a bore, but I managed to pee.

Zaki picked me up in his car, and we went off on errands—sorting out a bank loan for his friend and picking up new bedding from his dad's house. Zaki had moved into a flat opposite the kasbah only the day before. We took a stroll around the sounds and the smells of the cracked streets, listening to cats begging for the meat roasting on hot coals. There must be something more to this place that was, on the surface, devoid of its professed flowers, sport and divine favour.

"That big white mosque," I asked Zaki, "what's it called?"

"The White Mosque."

"Oh, right," I said, "like in that grand, local tradition of casas that are blanca?"

Silence.

We moved on to fruit smoothies and mixed-meat sandwiches. Perhaps the sandwich was a local speciality.

"No," said Zaki, "and it's just called a Mixed."

He didn't have much positive to say about Mohammedia, Morocco or anything.

Our desultory evening was conducted in French, "A beautiful language," he said, "but it's useless, and we're forced to use it at university."

He added, "But that's why the French were better colonialists than the Portuguese and the Spanish." I just nodded and smiled gravely, hoping the twitch in my eye wouldn't betray the unease I felt at being a touring Englishman having a conversation about colonialism.

We returned to his bare flat, and I settled into my sleeping bag on the bare floor. Conversation began to wilt in mutual weariness.

The rain continued to batter windows that refused to close because of poor hingemanship. Alas, my kit would still be wet in the morning. I fell asleep propped up on cushions by the window, gazing at the arched entrance to the kasbah—lit up in green and red I saw a Christmas tree and there found warmth beyond the rain. I hope Zaki did too.

—

On many days this walk felt no more than a prolonged attempt to coordinate bedtimes whilst maintaining a semblance of spontaneity and not wasting all my steps on the screen. I had chosen to leave camping as a last resort because I wanted to spend more time with people than the inside of my tent. Naturally introverted, I could easily walk for six months without talking to a soul, and all I'd have to show for it at the end would be half a haiku. (Though, if I'm honest / That could be more readable.)

Spend a day walking alone in silence to launch an outgoing, adventurous facade (read: has own moustache/wears down jacket) onto a series of students, families or out-of-work fishermen in cafés.

This was my opportunity to make fleeting lifelong connections, to find joy in encouraging others to be adventurous and, more importantly, to experience the humbling indifference that often comes with everyday encounters.

After all, I was always leaving tomorrow.

Zaki managed half a smile as I squelched out of his flat and downstairs for breakfast in the square below. I hit the jackpot with bread, avocado smoothie, coffee and a slice of laughing cow cheese on a plate drowned in olive oil and orange jam.

Today was the 6th of November, a national holiday for the Green March of 1975 when (in grossly over-simplified terms) a mass demonstration forced Spain to hand over the disputed territory of Western Sahara to Morocco. In some unplanned preparation for this day, I'd repeatedly listened to the song *Spanish Sahara* by Foals for the last week. It doesn't have much to do with the place. Still, the cathartic tempo as lead singer Yannis belts out a crescendo of furies is very let's-get-the-hell-out-of-this-town-at-dawn (while simultaneously being very let's-Google-greek-mythology-to-learn-what-furies-are-oh!-spirits-of-punishment-how-exciting!-how-apt!). It is just such internal tangents that frequently helped this pseud to break the never-ending loop of past-partner grooves and formative-years funk. "So I walked into the haze...." begins the song. And, in cold, damp clothes, I started the day's walk running out of an urban haze, heading, I hoped, for some rural sunshine.

Not long out of town, I was waved down by a man wearing a leather jacket so enormous I stopped only to see if he might be a real-life Morpheus from The Matrix. He stood close enough for me to count his bottom tooth and erupted into a diatribe against Morocco. He was spitting in French with bloodshot eyes. I was compelled to listen until he exhausted himself and began rocking back and forth on his feet, panting and, I was readily able to observe, dribbling.

The gist of his outburst was: "I hate the king." He seemed calmer now, so I assumed this was just something he needed to get out of his system to any passing stranger. I was beginning to feel like I might have to pat him on his leathered shoulder for reassurance when a bus suddenly appeared, perhaps by royal appointment. It slowed to a crawl, and the man smiled as if to communicate an apology, shook my hand, hopped aboard and was gone. I was left on the hard shoulder without even a blue pill to contemplate yet another oddity met by tarmac.

The day was spent trespassing a series of private beach resorts ranging from Happy Beach to Moonshine. Security guards cheered me along the sands and over fences. "Can I walk here?" I asked one as I clambered over yet another locked gate, "Ha ha ha!" he guffawed, "Bon périple!" Good trip! The guards were just grateful for activity in the absence of other tourists or anything that could be considered as having inspired the resort names.

In the early afternoon, I reached a long stretch of road that took me away from the coast and climbed a gentle rise. To my left green fields stretched to the sea, framing a solitary black cow in the distance. And on my right stood a row of women in wide straw hats selling some form of drink. By the time I'd reached the seventh woman, I felt more uncomfortable ignoring their calls than giving in and having some of what they were offering: milk. At least, that's what I understood from the word "laban," which in Egypt is just that, milk.

I was surprised when taking a carefree gulp of this Moroccan laban to discover it was fermented milk: slurpgurgleburp, and similar noises. I grinned at Woman Number Seven, who grinned back and refilled my glass, mistaking my shock for delight. Dairy products, like bedrooms, are something that Arabic dialects have little consensus on. But there's no use crying over milk, spilt, fermented or otherwise. And on I walked.

Arriving in Skhirat, I received a message from Yassine, my host for that evening, to say he had been forced to drive to Meknes in the north because his brother had been in a car accident. I sat in a café, feet throbbing and wondering what to do, listening to a father and teenage daughter eat eclairs beside me in silence. Half an hour later, I received another text from Yassine to say he was now driving back, overcome with a sense of duty to host me. I drank several bowls of soup over several hours and slept, slumped on the table. Father and daughter had gone by the time the waiter woke me up.

Yassine had had one hell of a day, so we went straight to his flat, a box on a roof, front door locked by a carefully propped broom handle. I wriggled into my damp sleeping bag and stretched out on the floor. We ate bread and cheese, drank tea and talked. Yassine was understandably glum, though thankfully his brother had not been hurt. He works as a counting assistant (one below an "assistant accountant," he was at pains to point out) for a clothing company, the Fruit of the Loom. He asked what I thought of Morocco, and I talked about my love of languages and history.

"Yes, that's what you tourists like," he said, "all Morocco has is history. There is no future."

He continued in the same vein for a while on the theme of life's woes. But, I proffered, your brother is fine, your job is not necessarily fruitless, nor does poverty immediately loom, etc. Unsurprisingly, he didn't see the funny side.

"You only see it like that because you're foreign," was his reply, and I daren't say he was right. And I daren't say anything to him about the sunsets either.

We fell asleep mid-conversation, and the Foals' song finally seemed relevant in the malaise of the last few days: "Forget the horror here / It's future rust and it's future dust."

—

Tourist or traveller. To move or to dwell. It rather depends on how much you enjoyed yesterday.

"Are you married? Am I beautiful?" said the waitress of the morning after.

Thankfully she left it at that, and I could drink my coffee in peace whilst scanning the day's route. Skhirat is several main roads plus a railway short of a shoreline, and I was in no mood to retrace my steps. It would be a morning marching inland in the shadow of dark clouds and a tunnel of trees. Around midday, I came to a deep gorge and a choice of two bridges. One was of the blocked-off, suspension sort, which I picked for the sheer thrill of it. Only when halfway across did I notice the rusted gaps in the floor and hurried as slowly as possible to the other side.

Once in the Rabat suburb of Temara, I sat at a terrace for m'semen drenched in thickly rich amlou (a dip made from argan oil, almonds and honey). A blissful moment of delicious, gloopy anonymity, no bag on my back, cats in various stages of disrepair meowing at my feet. The waft of commuters and the buzz of smoke.

As I sat there, a colourfully clad woman striding with purpose along the pavement suddenly fixed my vacant gaze: "Oh là là, it's *some*-body from some-*where* else," she said with the same em-*pha*-sis and without breaking step as she carried on into her day. She had summed up the mainstream of travel writing in one fell swoop of street theatre.

I soon hurried off, following a white butterfly into the heart of a slum—corrugated iron houses and bright laundry hanging from lines across the narrow streets; boys played marbles, and girls danced hopscotch in the dried mud.

There was no sense of accomplishment arriving in Rabat. It was my third time here in as many weeks, and I felt only inertia even though my existence had become defined by motion.

Here today and gone tomorrow. Tangier within a week, I determined.

Ali (my host for the night) lived in an upmarket neighbourhood across from a rocket science research centre. We chatted over lemon tea beside a sizeable bookcase. Ali revelled in speaking French rather than Arabic and aspired to become a writer and a bookseller. That evening he was to host a discussion group on "doctor-patient relationships." He handed me Henry Thoreau's Walking to read and went off to do some brain surgery, or some such.

What is it, what is it

But a direction out there,

And the bare possibility

Of going somewhere?

I slept, showered, scrubbed socks and dove into Thoreau for the rest of the day. His lines above recalled the aspirations that had first taken me to Agadir. Those bare possibilities! Look, mum, I'm going somewhere!

"You must walk like a camel," writes Thoreau, in a slight change of tone, "which is said to be the only beast which ruminates when walking." Terry Pratchett expanded on this with the observation that: "Camels are far too intelligent to admit to being intelligent" and "have that disdainful expression and famous curled lip as a natural result of an ability to do quadratic equations." Good for camels, I thought. Though camels have only made me seasick, walking as a human tends to provoke emptiness. I'd far rather disappear in geography than spit at geometry.

In the evening, I made a brief appearance to greet the mix of ex-pats and Moroccan doctors who made up the discussion group but took a French exit before they insisted I join them. With the door slightly ajar, I fell asleep to verbose talk of something that seemed so simple and human and, finally, wished I was a camel.

"Quick, get the banana in the photo!" Ali said, and we huddled in for a customary selfie at dawn. He began to pace up and down the kitchen, long night robe swishing about his ankles as he counted under his breath. He appeared to be in the middle of some great occult calculation before reaching a crescendo and declaring: "3,000 kilometres that's around 60,000 steps. Holy cow!"

A pep talk followed: "One step at a time, and you're already closer to home." Ali's infectious laugh, along with his animation, despite the hour, had me in unusually high spirits as I set off into the dark.

Eight kilometres of empty twilight along the tram lines to Salé, chewing banana and trying my hand (gut?) at ruminating. Over the river at sunrise, to my left, the kasbah bathed in the sleepy rays of dawn and through a large crack in Salé's old town wall. I kept on through the empty suburbs until the road became a muddy track twisting its way northward in the lee of the dunes.

My surroundings were soon dominated by workers in blue overalls and white hard hats. I weaved onwards for hours through a world of construction, wishing peace on all. A sour-faced foreman rode back and forth between the workstations, his large frame straddling a sagging old motorbike. And he studiously ignored me, back and forth, for the duration of the morning.

Shortly after I passed the last of the workers, a sharp screech suddenly drew my attention across a field. I saw a young girl dragging a dog along the track by its neck. I assumed the poor beast was dead until it let out a whine. The girl jumped out of her skin, let go of the lead and sprinted behind a farmyard wall. The dog shook itself and ambled off in the other direction as if it had all been but a game. The girl stood watching over a closed gate, plotting. I shouted some ineffectual curses in her general direction; she looked up and then slid back behind the wall. By now, the dog, too, had disappeared. The whole episode chilled me to the core, like a scene from a horror film utterly devoid of context.

I carried on, shuffling along on the tarmac under a relentless sun, wary of every possible girl and dog. The route gradually veered away from the coast, with no clear way back. I rested in a service-station café where the fog of smoke was more welcoming than the blank faces. Disfigures in the landscape. A few hundred metres later, I came to my first road marker for Tangier—240 kilometres away, it declared, half sunk in the ground and only partially legible. I knew the feeling.

I was utterly bored with the relentless honking of the main road. Google Maps showed a possible off-road shortcut, so I took an inspired turn straight into a maze at the village of Sidi Taibi. I was soon utterly disorientated in the narrow alleys and stopped by a doorstep to reassess.

The comforting smell of freshly baked bread wafted from somewhere nearby. Children played football in the street; men trundled over potholes on motorbikes, and women walked past, staring under mountains of bags. A head popped out from a window near my feet. It was covered in flour and had a ball of dough in one hand. It turned out I was sitting outside a basement bakery. The baker came out and was unfazed by my being there; he simply gave me some bread and pointed the way out of the village past the purple mosque and onto Kenitra.

A white pickup truck appeared beyond the purple mosque and drew level for a group of men in the trailer to yell something at me before speeding away into the dust. Who'd enraged them? The generous baker, perhaps, the colour of the mosque, this audacious transient? Or, more likely, it was a variation on the "somebody from somewhere else" theme. A man on a bicycle appeared from the settling dust cloud and asked if the men had bothered me. I thanked him for his concern, and he pedalled off to where a white police car lurked under the boughs of a large tree.

I watched from afar as an officer pulled over the pick-up truck and exploded at the men in violent gestures. Soon after, the officers also stopped the man on the bicycle. He motioned in my direction, they nodded, and he carried on. When I finally plodded up to the tree, the officers merely waved me on from their car window without even an oh là là. Proof that by the very act of walking, problems go away. Mainly because it takes so bloody long to get anywhere that by the time you arrive, the problem has buggered off somewhere else.

The track passed a shanty town of make-shift, corrugated iron shacks, each adorned with a large satellite dish. Cats and cattle, side by side, feasting on skips that spilt out all the way to the two obelisks of Kenitra's gateway. "We wish the honourable visitor a happy stay in the city," were the words written on the base.

Something rhythmic this way comes. I could hear chattering from ahead where a mass of police hovered in the margins. Turning the corner, I ran into a large crowd of teenagers in school uniforms marching along the road. As we bobbed along, I gradually began to understand what they were chanting: "A-ssha'b ureed isqaat a-ssa'a"—"The People Demand the

Fall of the Hour!" sung to a chant made famous during the 2011 uprisings (replace "hour" with "regime"). I turned to a member of the fringes and asked what the issue was.

"They want to get rid of the king," he said.

Another man told him to shut up and said to me:

"No, they want the clocks to change to wintertime."

I learnt through a hushed conversation with man number two that the king had made a snap decision the day before not to change the clocks back for winter this year, or ever again.

"It was a stupid decision," said the second man.

"And will it change?"

"Of course not."

Team Winter was made up almost exclusively of teenagers in high spirits. They were far outnumbered by Team Let's Watch From the Side Lines And See What Happens. Winter came all the same: rain blew in on a gusting wind, and I hid under an awning to wait until my host, Ayoub, finished work. A few hours over nuss-nuss and journal. The demonstrators continued to march in anti-clockwise laps of the streets, passing my spot every 20 minutes or so, their number ever diminishing. The other lone men of the wooden chairs merely watched them blankly and without comment.

All of a sudden, I was addressed amidships by an American accent under a Panama hat:

"You from England?" it said. I looked up, and a man was standing on the pavement before me in a vision of khaki.

"Yes."

"Don't go to America," he said, "S'all money and violence."

"Um, thanks, but why?"

"Just don't go there, all right!" he said, and just as quickly as he'd materialised, he melted back into the crowd.

There's a proverb, whose attribution somewhat dubiously spreads from Morocco to Afghanistan, that points its finger at the West and says: "You have the watches, we have the time." It felt rather appropriate on this of all days. There was something amiss with time today—strange episodic moments with girls, dogs, and men shouting, all culminating in these confounded circumambulations against the clocks.

I settled into my chair and thought of how someone once summed up the works of Chaucer: "Intended to impress rather than inform, and is, in fact, the more impressive the less it is understood." That should do it, I thought, and lente backe againste the walle of the steepede establishmente, revellinge inne thise tayle of myne, waitinge fore bedetime.

9

Me duelen los pies

("My feet hurt," Spanish, key phrases of which
I'd now started to learn)

A FEW WEEKS BEFORE LEAVING Cairo, I posted about
my walk in an Arab travel group on Facebook.
I'd hoped for advice and to find Moroccans to
stay with along the way. Thousands replied.
Though the vast majority responded only to
praise my "stupidity" for being "yet another
European with time too much time on his
hands": take a plane, mate, and piss off home.
That was their general idea. Point taken, to
some extent. Privilege aside, the subtext was an
aversion to exercise and people doing things
differently.

Nonetheless, some kind souls offered
suggestions, and others even offered me a bed
for the night. Ayoub from Kenitra was one of the
latter and was true to his word. He found me at
the café, and we walked through the remnants
of the winter protest to his parent's home in the

old town, surrounded by the aromas of baking and damp.

Over a casse-croûte of pastries, Ayoub talked about two of his friends who had drowned off the coast of Portugal the previous summer trying to reach Europe (a phenomenon called hareeg—"burning"). They'd made it up the coast along the popular smuggling route, avoiding detection beyond the horizon and over the strait before their boat flipped and sank.

"Islack" was the Darija word he used to describe life in Kenitra. Neither good nor bad. Dreams of Europe but not of burning. I decided to take the next day off to rest my loins and to let the lingering confusions from the previous few days catch up with their narrator before tackling the final stretch to Tangier.

We spent the evening at a café with Ayoub's cousin Ahmed and Ahmed's girlfriend, the waitress (I forget, or perhaps never knew, her name). We watched football and the motions of a lump in Ahmed's top lip. He caught me staring at it and curled his lips to reveal a wad of black gooey hashish called kaala. The evening progressed and was positively islack, everyone was cold, and it was clear we'd only come out as wingmen for Ahmed.

I've never been much of a football fan, so my attention lingered on Ahmed as he sat there gormless as a colourless parrotfish, with a protruding lip and reddening eyes, gradually becoming more and more sedated as the kaala dissolved. All the while, his intended busied around with coffees, teas and broomsticks. And, wait, yes! Now I could see it: she, too, had the tell-tale bump on her lip. Ah, romance! Eventually, I got a headache and went to bed under about five blankets to have nightmares about evil girls playing with dogs and time.

I awoke to muted giggling as Ayoub left for work and Ahmed arrived home. I heard Ahmed say in a hushed voice that his motorbike had broken down in the middle of the night somewhere outside of town, so he and his girlfriend had had to walk back through the forest, alone. More giggles. Then there was the faintest suggestion of a high-five before the door clicked shut.

I retreated under the covers to surface several hours later in search of breakfast at the café. There, I met Ahmed and his girlfriend in an exchange of winks. As he proudly told me, Ahmed is known locally as "Chinwi" because his friends say he looks Asian. I'd begun to think of him as progressive. We spent the morning doing nothing but watching the men across the street in another café who were also doing nothing. So in a way, we were all doing something.

School children came and went in twos and threes, still singing yesterday's chant for winter. The sun made a spirited appearance between the rain to mark the persistence of summer. Eventually tired of the Long Gaze, Ahmed fired up his now miraculously mended bike and zoomed off to attend a funeral. Ayoub turned up early from work, saying he had left because of toothache, and set about soothing the pain with sweet mint tea. Hair of the dog and all that.

"For me, travel is life," he said as we walked along the beach, a short taxi ride down the hill. We ate doughnuts on the sand as the sun set over a turbulent sea below a tiny and forlorn kasbah. Despite the rough waters, I felt inordinately calm after an exhausting week and the prospect of reaching Spain in a week. I found a peace enhanced by Ayoub's enthusiasm (and in defiance of his toothache that gave him a resting wince face). I asked what he'd say to someone who wanted to visit Kenitra:

"Ahla wa sahla" (welcome). This is a less pointed gambit than what the obelisks promised. Though, the more I thought about it, the more it rang true to his modesty: Welcome to Kenitra! Come, see it for yourself! (Or perhaps he just hadn't understood my question.) I now faced two days of empty coastline with no towns or villages. I could only pray the dunes would be welcoming for a night à la belle étoile.

After breakfast, Ayoub walked me to a little bridge beyond the old town. In Moroccan Arabic, "little bridge" would be "kenitra," however, the town of Kenitra (despite all the evidence) is not named after this bridge. Rather annoyingly for everyone involved, the little bridge of the town's name was destroyed in 1928.

Ayoub plied me with a load of ballutah (large acorns) bought from a woman guarding a massive pile of the things on the pavement. We parted ways at the little bridge—"a laboratory of movements, tones, shapes, contrasts, rhythms, and the relations between all of these," reads a critique of De Brug, and this was echoed in my little bridge of Kenitra. Oh, what it is to be a gallivanting pseud with unlimited internet! Off I went along the main road, popping acorns as I trod and itching to make friends, now as Ibn *Ballutah*. The morning's company was in the storks, clacking in pairs from bulging nests atop telephone poles.

Near the end of the first village, three girls came a-skipping from behind, "Monsieur! Monsieur!" they said. All in their school uniform, with black hair, long past their shoulders, wide grins and bulging cheeks. Colourful backpacks slung over their shoulders.

"What's your name?" said one in French.

I replied in my best Darija and asked theirs.

"Nour," "Halima," "Huria," they said, before adding in chorus, "we are ten years old."

"Why are you in Morocco? Huria said in Classical Arabic, "Is it to learn a new language and to discover a different culture and its people?"

From a little bridge to three little thrills of a grand morning. I could have hugged her. I was so excited about their curiosity. But I was attracting enough suspicion as a foreign man who appeared to be leading three girls out of the village.

We walked on, and Huria (whose name is Arabic for "freedom") asked me about my life, what I had learned at school and what England was like. Not long later, we arrived at a fork in the road where they joined for a "goodbye" in English, then ran off in a muddle of hands, bags and pigtails.

I turned down the other fork along a track that I hoped would lead to the sea and straight away ran into a parked police car. The officer in charge (him with the biggest hat) checked my passport, drew himself up to the full width of his brim and dispensed some official travel advice:

"Don't speak to anyone unless they are in uniform and only sleep in hotels."

I relished the thought that, at that very moment, Nour, Halima and Huria were relating their morning encounter to their classmates. Big Hat confirmed that the track does indeed end at the beach. And I assured him that, naturally, I was booked into a hotel for the night, only, being an absentminded tourist, I couldn't remember the name of either the town or the hotel. The officer with the smaller hat suggested a place that sounded vaguely familiar (though significantly inland), and I agreed that it was indeed my destination. Thus reassured, officers big and small hat waved me on my way.

Hitting the beach, I turned right and walked towards where the cliffs vanished into the mist, aiming for a wood some 50 kilometres from Kenitra. No hotels there, Mr Big Hat. With every kilometre, I'd pass a small white building with boarded-up windows. Fisherman's huts, I assumed and walked on.

I saw not a soul all morning—just endless sands towards a horizon, all a haze with the crashing waves. The sun was due to set in around five hours, and I was covering good ground, hoping to be zipped up and cosy long before nightfall. Then, as I approached yet another fisherman's shack, three dogs suddenly charged down from a ridge. I saw them off with stones, then came a man's voice, crisp and alert:

"Stop. Moroccan army." Two men emerged from the shack in pyjamas, unsmiling and brandishing walkie-talkies. They marched towards me and I dropped the stones, surreptitiously (I hoped), behind my feet.

"Who are you?" said one, "What are you doing here? This is a military zone."

I explained with as much enthusiasm and reference to Ibn Battutah (I'd run out of acorns) as I could muster. They nodded along with my story, and there was the growing hint of a smile that began to betray suspicion, which, on its way to understanding, took a sudden stop at bewilderment.

"Where are you sleeping tonight?"

Best to be honest, I thought, and told them about the intended woods. To my relief, this registered no alarm.

"Ok. Just make sure you're off the beach by night."

They were the guards of the sea and the shacks their watchtowers. This stretch of coastline is prime for drug running, they warned. Information that was tantamount to being told, "here be pirates." I was unsure what to do with it apart from finding bigger stones. They insisted on taking a selfie then I was allowed to carry on.

Daylight was fading fast and I was running out of time to reach the wood before sunset. Now that the news had gotten out, I was stopped at each post by dogs and soldiers. Time and nerves were both beginning to slip. Eventually, I suggested to one soldier (if you don't mind, possibly, please, dear God, etc.) that he pass a message down the line to say that I wasn't a pirate or carrying drugs so that I wouldn't have to stop and explain myself every ten minutes.

At the next, a man dressed in what I'd come to recognise as "Moroccan army chill" (flip-flops, green jacket and grey tracksuit trousers) waved me over.

"There's been talk on the radio of someone of your description walking along these parts."

This was more of a passing statement over the garden fence than a question. I leant over to concur and to add a "what say you pal that I keep moving before I lose sight of my own feet and you can go back to sleep." He said no for the same reason and instructed me to head directly inland. A simple matter, he implied, of crossing a short stretch of dunes and following the motorway till it meets a service station, then I'd find the forest on the other side. I couldn't say no since, despite the flip-flops, he was carrying a rifle.

Nature writer Robert Macfarlane talks exquisitely of walking as a journey through exterior and interior landscapes. He likens metaphor to being the service station of a walker's inner landscape. My exterior was barbed-wire fences and dodging trucks on the service station slip road.

A simple matter, indeed. I was drenched in sweat, and my nerves were shot to pieces in the hard shoulder as the sun set over the pumps of my fabled metaphor. I strode through gatherings of families dining in the picnic area. Mutterings and gasps followed in my wake. All I wanted was to hide among the mental shrubbery of my inner landscape ablaze with desperate hopes of sleep.

Now wedged on a ridge, I was lit up by headlights hurtling along a motorway. You never feel so overt as when trying to be covert. Beyond endless poly tunnels concealing twilight shadows of man-eating triffids (no doubt, these were harmless bananas by day). Gradually the air changed as a dense covering of trees arose around me, vague in the dim light. Ducking under a small footbridge, I almost marched straight into a donkey cart. The two men with the reigns studiously ignored my greeting as they trundled past, and I hurried on, trying to affect an air that I was heading for my little cottage in the woods.

Before long, all was perfectly black. I stumbled around until I found a suitable thicket and fashioned a dog-proof fence out of a mesh of branches. I opted for the quick and noiseless bivvy bag rather than the faff and rustle of a tent.

My body steamed, and my mind fumed with a cocktail of adrenaline and frustration. A dog barked nearby, and thoughts strayed to the two men on the cart. But there was no use dwelling on uncertainties as I locked myself up in my sleeping bag and lay under an open canopy of constellations. Finally warm and safe, I drifted off at "the crossroads of forests, where paths converge under the leaves. Who would I meet in the stars?" so said adventurer/philosopher Sylvain Tesson. And no amount of barking could spoil being drowsy in nature.

I awoke drenched and with something warm and furry on my forehead. It squeaked at my twitches and scuttled off into the undergrowth. A little mouse had found warmth and safety on my face. It hadn't rained, so my sweat must've condensed inside the bivvy. And then rained on me. I lay there trying to ignore the growing chill in the small hours before dawn until the first cockerel crowed and the milky way returned to the night. A donkey joined in, and it was time to gather my things and go after the mouse into the new day. The world was a hazy pink behind a thick fog slowly enveloping the forest. I floundered in various directions until, at last, I could follow the sound of lorries back to the failed metaphor of yesterday.

Nothing to see here, just a boy beyond the trees. Back into the wilds of the pumps, where an employee stopped me and was instantly lost for words. To save him the awkwardness of asking if I took petrol or diesel, I bade him a cheery hello and asked the way to the road.

Rather than face further questions from soldiers on the coast, I decided to walk inland to the mouth of the estuary at Moulay Bousselham. The day's intrigue was the possibility of being defeated by another river. I walked on autopilot, hoping for magical fish or another green man. I was utterly fed up with smiling and waving at empty faces. There are only so many times you can wish peace upon someone and mean it.

Sometime after midday, a bored barber basking in the blazing sun called me over for tea. I'd officially become an amigo rather than a monsieur, though I preferred the latter, to be frank (lol). Mohammed's barber shop had seemingly been designed after a road accident: seat ripped from a car (complete with seat belt) and rear-view mirrors used as, well, mirrors. He sat on the floor behind a gas burner and, with sebsi in hand, plied me with hot bread and melted butter. I sipped and munched as he puffed and sipped. When I stood to leave, he called to his children and three random men outside to join us for a photo. Under the pressure of an audience, I showed them how I drink water from my CamelBak and to my horror, they all lined up for a trial suck.

There was nothing spiritual at the shoreline. There was only a man looking to make a fast buck who shepherded me into a small wooden boat away from a queue of locals waiting for the regular ferry. He took me across for a fee I probably owed Mother Nature for last night's lodgings. The houses of Moulay Bousselham in reds, blues, yellows and beiges glittered up a hilltop over green banks. I pitched my tent on the far side in the shade of a row of French camper vans.

That evening, I stalked the narrow and crowded alleys atop the hill, slipping on upturned buckets of octopus and searching for a steaming bowl of harira. Once found, I washed it down with chicken tajine and banana juice to spite the triffids of the previous night's polytunnels. The sun set behind the bulging estuary as the crescent moon rose over yesterday's woods against a sky of darkest violet. I hoped for another safe forehead for the mouse that night. Down by the banks, the lingering sogginess of my sleeping bag was no match for the heaviness of my eyelids.

10

"I do what I like most of the time and I feel low-level bad about it most of the time too."

Liam Williams, *Homes and Experiences*

I WOKE UP BESIDE A CAT that had found its way through both layers of the tent to shelter by my head. We awoke simultaneously and looked at each other for a moment before the cat darted out the (but-I'd-definitely-zipped-it-up) unzipped entrance and into the wet dawn. Yesterday a mouse, today a cat. I packed the tent and made my way up the hill for breakfast with the prospect of a dog on my forehead tomorrow.

"Good morning, khawaga!" said the waiter with an animation that clashed with the quiet morning chill as he descended with a tray of coffee, orange juice, three dates and a warm bowl of white harira.

Khawaga is an Egyptian way of addressing foreigners. Everyday over-the-counter banter in Cairo. It's a rib-tickling nod at the "you're not from around here, how interesting that must be for you" tradition. It comes from a Persian term denoting a Sufi teacher, and I like to kid myself that that's what they really mean—esoteric is the Egyptian of the streets.

Hesitant layabout, I've lived abroad for most of my twenties and have become accustomed to being outed as a stranger before breakfast. Nevertheless, I'd hoped to maintain my cover today since I would be heading back into the military zone.

I hung around at the café until the hour seemed reasonable enough to feasibly defend not having camped in the dunes (for some reason, I thought this would be in my favour) and hoped the soldiers would take me for a wandering dervish, or failing that, a foreigner.

The first post passed in silence; the only sound was the smooth crunch of soft sand. The sky was an exhibition of greys, and a tempest raged over the ocean. Soon into the morning, a low grumble of engines came from up ahead, obscured beyond the dunes. The ground gradually levelled out, and the sand turned into a coarse, reddish-brown expanse crisscrossed with deep, weaving tracks and pockets of men digging holes into a dim horizon.

Long queues of trucks lined the tracks; their trailers piled high with sand. Here falling into step behind a train of donkeys, there behind a tumbling trail of tyres as high as my chest. Men stuffed sand into bags hung over the donkeys' necks, booting and whipping the poor beasts up steep gullies from the sea. I jostled among the trucks in their vast lines between the makeshift quarries. I had no idea what I was walking through, there being no distinction between the formal and the informal, but I nonetheless opted for a smile and a wave and was responded to in kind.

Most likely, it was an informal (#illegal) sand mining operation. That is to say, a lucrative business for making cement is run by so-called "sand-mafias." The sand is purloined, en masse, from the more remote beaches (the coastal soldiers appear to turn a blind eye) and shipped off to build fancy hotels for tourists. It's an operation aimed at improving tourism while at the same time devastating Morocco's main tourist attraction: the beach.

I dodged donkeys and greeted hundreds of bemused drivers and distracted workers over the day. Nobody stopped me or questioned my presence. I guess we were in it together in the camaraderie of illicitness. At one point, a sand mafioso, leaning on his shovel, beckoned me over to marvel at his shrivelled left eye and a long zig-zag scar down one cheek.

"I got it in a knife fight!" he said with a crooked smile before adding, "do you have a knife?"

I did indeed. At the top of my side pocket, resting by my right hand, just waiting for him to yell, "draw!" I reckoned it prudent to deny this and that the appropriate response would be: "Say, what's a knife?"

"There are dangerous people about. You should carry one," he said, gesturing around him with the shovel. The other men didn't look up but dug on in earnest.

As I stood there, a little anxious, I happily recalled Theroux's *Tao*—of reading a novel unrelated to the place you are in—and sought reassurance in another passage from *Lint* when the titular writer's marriage begins to falter "due to his attempt to pass off a sleep-crease as a glamorous knife-scar." So, for lack of any evidence to the contrary, I transformed this man into an overslept and estranged cult author moonlighting as a sand thief. We exchanged silent smiles, and I slowly legged it round the corner.

It was hours and hours through crowds of greetings until the quarries eventually returned to gentle dunes, military posts and charging dogs. And so the day continued, with a firm grasp on my stick and a mind on nearby stones. Occasionally a soldier could be heard, muffled, calling off the dogs as I passed. But only twice did anyone bother to investigate the cause of the barking. Some shacks had cats rather than dogs; they yawned and stretched in defiance. At the final post before Larache, a soldier came out in full uniform and ordered that I explain myself. Ignoring my half-hearted mention of Ibn Battutah, he pointed over my shoulder:

"What's that on your bag?"

I pivoted and posed, Gore-Tex manakin:

"A waterproof cover."

"What's it for?"

"To stop the rain getting in my bag."

"Why?"

"Because I don't want my things to get wet."

"What's that writing?"

"Osprey, it's the brand name."

"But what does it mean?"

"It's a type of bird, but they also make bags."

"But why?"

"Some people feel the rain, others just get wet," is a quote variously attributed to Roger Miller, Bob Dylan or Bob Marley. The lesser-known ending to this doubtful aphorism, attributed to no one in particular, goes: "And still there are others who feel the need to make sure that it's you who gets wet." The rain had begun to fall in thick sheets as the conversation became about as pointless as my waterproofs. He wasn't armed, so I turned and walked off into Larache, ignoring his shouts that were soon lost in the deluge. I entered the first café and sat down with a puddle. Heads turned in a collective shudder.

"Sorry. A thief has stolen my phone," came the ping of a message from my supposed host for the night. The subtext (it took me many cold hours to interpret) was that the hosting was now cancelled. To hell with interaction.

This is precisely the state of mind that the exercise of staring from café terraces exists to solve. If only out of fear of becoming part of the wall, Davy Jones' Locker-like, I slowly gathered the inclination to ask the waiter what a lone, "Bootstraps" Battutah has to do for a bed in these parts. He directed me to a hotel on nearby

Ibn Battutah Street, and this coincidental fact cheered me up inordinately.

I ducked into the doorway of what had once clearly been a grand townhouse: tall ceilings and colourful mosaic tiles. A small man in a brown suit sprang from a room to the right of the entrance.

"Hello! I'm a retired religious professor," he said by way of introduction, bowing slightly, "Jamal al-Din al-Larachi, is the name, after the great Islamic scholar Jamal al-Din al-Afghani."

His Arabic lilted with Spanish, and he added the odd word in French to emphasise the ends of his disparate clauses. It was a struggle to follow his flow as he launched into a polyglot monologue about widespread illiteracy before concluding how it's a shame that nobody listens anymore. I nodded throughout in the hope that he would get his own point.

"My name means: 'the beauty of religion'," he continued before changing key, suddenly, into a rendition of The Bare Necessities, hips swaying like Baloo. I made for the stairs as he morphed once more into singing "goodnight mate, goodnight mate" to me in some not-readily-discernible samba-style tune. I turned at the top step to see him mincing a one-person hip wiggle back across the hallway.

At least someone had found bliss in the day's blues. There was far too much going on in the footnotes of this day for a sleepy mind to unpack without help from the dream world. I retreated to a room overlooking the street that was now a steady brook and hung my gear from all available surfaces. It was a jungle out there, as well as in here. I slept fully clothed under several towels and blankets, surrounded by dripping.

Shadows of lone men hurried along the alleys, huddled inside the deep hoods of long djellabas—tips firm in the nip of dawn. I joined with collar up and woollen hat low.

At some arbitrary point on the Atlantic coast, say around a service station near a forest a day's walk from Kenitra, the Moroccan attitude towards milk violently shifts. South of this point, when one orders a nuss-nuss, the espresso shot is poured directly onto the milk creating a swirl of murmurations as the two liquids meet like a poetic prelude in a bubbling dual of dairy and bean. You're sat at the terrace contemplating your creeping insignificance or, more likely, that of the chap across the way who's doing precisely the same as you.

In contrast, north of this forest, the milk is brought to the table and poured directly onto the coffee—creating what can only be described as a glass of hot brown. Such a cavalier attitude to dairy is perhaps what people meant when they said to watch out for those in the north. Milk, coffee, bosh, stare, insignificance. Or just that the nuss-nuss is to Morocco what the scone is to England. A storm both in a teacake and in a teacup.

Concerned at my growing pedantry, I downed the brown without comment and walked down the hill and out of town. Today's air was light and clean, with nothing to see of yesterday's rain.

"You've walked by foot from Agadir?" said the policeman on the bridge down from Larache, "that's impossible."

"I'm walking by foot to Tangier. Is that possible?"

He held my eye as he considered this.

"Yes, I suppose it is."

"But from Agadir, that's impossible? You don't believe me?"

"No, not at all."

He thought some more, settled on an emphatic wave and wished my feet well for the road. Onwards I continued among the hard shoulder society of national route one: sheep, goats, shepherds side-saddle on donkeys and colourfully dressed women with arms full of fruit, piously ignored.

I walked a marathon that day through gentle green valleys and hilltop villages dotted about in a landscape that could have been Tuscan. I stopped for bread and cheese by a mosque with a blue and white minaret and watched a man complete a set of star jumps, a blustering sail in his djellaba. Once finished, he sat beside me and lit a cigarette. The smoke curled high up into the canopy of the trees. He spoke of the Moroccan coast and how there's nowhere in the world he'd rather live. He gestured to the grassland that stretched for miles down to the deep blue ocean before us, and I knew what he meant.

Towards mid-afternoon, two shepherd boys clocked me from a field. Sniggering to one another, they began goading a snapping dog and lobbing stones at me. I cursed and threw stones back at them, for the trio only to come on louder. I crossed a busy road to get away and swore at the cars and lorries too. The rest of the day was downcast, and dismal was my arrival in Asilah as I slumped into a chair at the central Café Meknes.

My (intended) host for that night (in Asilah) messaged me to say: "Oh, by the way, I live in Tangier." But he nonetheless hoped I'd enjoy my stay in Asilah—nice kasbah, restaurants, beach, etc.

Ah, hope.

"Everyone means well when they are making promises to strangers," says the poet Matt Bayliss, and god, how I hate it when the poets are right. With their floppy hair and their adverbs.

I was almost at the end of my tether. Not a poet. Barely a walker. I was a day's walk from Tangier, the end of the Moroccan stage of my walk, and had completely lost sight of what had put me on this trail in the first place.

I had nothing to go back to. Nothing in Cairo and nothing in England. Give me the ease of Europe, I thought then.

And, as if to complete this first-world pincer movement, my iPhone—source of navigation and distraction—stopped working.

Ffyona Campbell faced stone throwing and sexual harassment daily when she walked through Morocco in the early 1990s. Her account is harrowing and highlights what remains the privilege of travelling as a lone man. That, and her phenomenal character. Like me, she hails from the southwest of England and I hoped there was something of her spirit in those Westcountry waters like there wasn't in the waters around Tangier. (As will become clear in the next few pages.) Must do better, I said through gritted teeth.

When I eventually emerged from the darkest reaches of my traveller's funk, I tried my luck with the waiter. He wasn't keen on me sleeping in the café but directed me instead to a hotel where, he *was* keen to tell me, he also worked. But I took a room anyway and spent the evening washing my socks and grimacing.

I found enthusiasm enough to head out for two soul-warming bowls of harira through Donkey Gate at the entrance to an old town of old-hat blues and whites. I sipped the soup, still feeling low-level bad about this whole non-adventure, and watched as the bright pink sky filled with hundreds of starlings. Life shimmered in an array of fluid shapes as they swooped and rippled. An infinity of possibilities flashed across their abstract frames. Damn them and their effortlessness, I thought. The sublime only enraged me further, and I swore at the waiter when he demanded a tip for the effort of bringing me bread. The night was restless in burning feet, and I regretted not taking a third bowl of soup.

It's "life for life's sake," wrote Paul Bowles, "in the meantime you eat."

11

"Tangier was famous for three things—its grapes, its pears, and the brainlessness of its inhabitants."

Abu 'l-Fida, 14th-century geographer.

IT WAS SEVEN IN THE MORNING at Café Meknes. I was drinking coffee in the dark when a man appeared with a spliff drooping from his bottom lip and tried to sell me a flat. On he went, breaching the fragile peace gradually settling in my thoughts, spurting a repertoire of languages to see which sparked a reaction. In Egyptian, I told him, as calmly as possible, that I never rent property before breakfast.

"Oh, you're Turkish!" he said in French. Meanwhile, the waiter smiled in Absolute Idiot as he wiped the tables around us.

"No, I'm not," I said in English.

"¡Pero, amigo!"

He continued in Spanish until I stood up and snarled at him in High Pitched. The waiter took the man by the elbow and led him inside, both beside themselves with laughter. I dropped some coins on the table and marched straight out of town in a festering mood, forgetting, in all the commotion, to pick up bread and cheese. I'd also run out of dates. No matter, I would walk on water and frustration—a remarkably potent combination that saw me the final fifty kilometres to Tangier. There aren't enough hours in the day to be annoyed. But there are enough to walk.

Every distant bark had my nerves on edge, and my temper was reflected in those I met along the way. An elderly lady hovering by the roadside saw me approaching and instantly made to cross. Unfortunately for her, I'd already had the same idea. Our eyes met across the middle of an empty road, and hers shone with horror. With a muted shriek, she turned and hastened away, muttering curses and hexes in her wake. Hours later, I encountered a woman in a similar predicament, leaning against a wheelbarrow piled with melons. I offered to help, thrusting my arms to motion pushing, but she shooed me away, adding a gruff "shame on you" in Arabic. As I walked on in my shame, it dawned on me that my mime must have seemed, well, incredibly unseemly.

As I reached the far end of a dehydrated blur, and in the middle of an area my map claimed to be "The Diplomatic Forest," a man pulled alongside me in a truck to ask whether I was Muslim. He shadowed me for ten minutes sprouting alleged Qur'anic proverbs before giving up and speeding off in a cloud of diplomacy. We must've been nearing the spring of Baqal, which Abu 'l-Fida cites as the source of the foolishness of Tangerines.

Past Ibn Battouta [sic] airport and several Ibn Battutah warehouses for coffee and (mineral) water at an Ibn Batouta [sic] petrol station. Tangier being Ibn Battutah's birthplace, the inconsistent transliterated spellings of his name showed a varied taste but hinted at a limited palette.

There's a saying about Tangier that you cry when you leave and you cry when you arrive. And indeed, I proved the first half of this true as I became a snivelling mess of shooting pains along the main drag into town. The road was lined with enormous Moroccan flags, which a better re-writer would have at least found significant, even if after the fact.

But my thoughts pooled with the blood in my feet as I hobbled along the cobbles. I'd managed to get my phone to partially charge, but only when turned off. I don't know if I was more annoyed at this failure of technology or that it proved my dependency on it. As I walked, I saw only the nearest faces and the most distant buildings. If I had been able to take photos, they would have been of my ankles.

Late in the afternoon, I slumped onto the grass by the Syrian mosque below Charf Hill— said to be the burial ground of the giant Antaeus after Hercules killed him. Sure, along with the mosque's needle-like minaret, it was as good a place as any for a defeat. Almost immediately, my host Soufian found me and declared triumphantly: "Hey, you with the green bag!" beaming a smile of pure and utter human warmth. And just like that, with a simple and heartfelt gesture, the woes pressing me down were lifted—here was the ending I'd wished for.

We took a shared taxi back to the malodorous slopes of east Tangier. Soufian talked animatedly in the cramped space about all the foreigners he'd hosted over the years and how it was his only means of travelling: through the experiences of others. His house was deep in a tangled tenement of rubbish and cats.

Here, shoes off and ensconced on cushions, I could celebrate my Moroccan end. I was far from the sullen mood of the morning now and had my own personal vat of spicy harira. Soufian's toddler brother Anis crawled around my feet pretending to be a goat, his bleats between my blisters, and I made nonsense noises at him until Soufian left for a night shift at a factory near Ibn Batouta airport. I fell asleep and didn't wake up until noon the following day.

I was woken by Anis advancing on all fours over my legs, braying. I sat up, pulled various blankets around me and blinked for the first time at a map of Spain. I stared at it with much the same unease as I'd first stared at the map of Morocco. Spain was rather big.

Breakfast upstairs with Soufian's mum, dad and aunt. An assortment of bread, bowls of olive oil, grapes and pears, glasses of tea and familiar sugar-frosted biscuits shaped like zeroes that I'd last seen with the mathematicians of Agadir. In my end is my, um, nothing.

I mentioned Ibn Battutah and Soufian's dad responded with an array of exclamations that reached such levels as: "Didn't we learn about him at school? Great man..., went to China," before picking up a parallel train of thought:

"I knew a man once who walked from Marrakech to Tangier," he said as if remembering a dream.

"Why did he do that?" I asked.

"Because he couldn't afford the bus," he said, hitching up his striped djellaba to show me a pair of cracked ankles. And, with a wiggle of his toes and a change of pronoun, he continued, "when I arrived, my feet were so swollen I couldn't take off my shoes."

Is it only us hopeless romantics who consider walking anything more than a mere inconvenience?

I took the bus into town for my first glimpse across at Tarifa and the high ridge I would soon climb as my initial steps in Europe. But before I did, I wanted to pay my respects at the tomb of Ibn Battutah, which lay somewhere in the depths of the kasbah.

I stopped first by Café Tingis to try and charge my blinkered phone. European digital nomads on laptops sat spaced between the tiles and the locals. Each seeking their slice of the beat generation, spread on toast, smashed avocado like, in the world of a Burroughs naked brunch. Anxious that I was giving the impression that I, too, had come to write a cut-up sonnet comparing a tangerine to a Seville orange, I drank my coffee in silence and frowned at the wall.

A man with a leather satchel and moth-eaten shoes weaved between the tables selling individual cigarettes. The waiter in a white shirt, black waistcoat and tie looked like he'd come with the foundations. He switched on the TV in the corner, and the screen flickered onto live footage of French President Macron and King Mohammed VI smiling as they were escorted through Tangier train station. They shook hands and waved at ticket machines as they prepared to inaugurate a new high-speed train. The café around me steadily filled up for the momentous occasion—chatter, tension, smoke. There were audible gasps as the commentator reeled off the facts.

"Tangier to Kenitra in fifty minutes!"

"Casablanca in two hours!"

One man was so moved that he erupted in spontaneous applause when the train left the station. But when a close-up of the driver revealed him to be, beyond doubt, a white Frenchman, there was an immediate furore. The digital nomads scribbled some lines they could pass off later as insight (I was there, man

/ I could smell history). Others hid under their Panama hats. Lost and confused as to where my loyalties lay, I continued staring at the wall. Once all had settled, both King and President back to beaming at ticket barriers and exposed plumbing, the crowds gradually filtered out, and the waiter, in a wonderful feat of irony, switched the channel over to Meg Ryan in French Kiss.

I longed to spend weeks lounging on the balconies of timeless Tangier. Where glimpses of the Spanish coast are half caught between the narrows and the shadows across the great Levanter wind. Thus inspired, I took several random turns beyond the café and entered Pension Agadir (on a whim, because of the name) to ask the rate for the night. A man in long johns told me it would be the equivalent of three English pounds.

Perhaps I'd stay a few days, I thought. To settle lingering woes and heal festering toes. But then, I knew I had to make some progress through Spain before winter set in. There was still a long way to go. And, judging by the ambient vibrations from within, guests at Pension Agadir were expected to die noisily in their sleep.

—

I sat for an hour with my back to Ibn Battutah's tomb. A small and simple white dome on a hidden corner of the kasbah. It was locked, and I was alone. Down by the harbour front, the travel agents prefer to market themselves after Marco Polo while Ibn Battutah lies lost in a twist of passageways, found within, not from without. Now that's style.

"You know what? I've just scaled the Maghreb," was the thought that popped into my head. It was a line I'd once overheard in Amman, Jordan, where I studied for a year. Said by a Hooray Henry type when a Regular Joe would've simply said, "I've been to Morocco." He pronounced "Maghreb" as if talking about the matriarch of some Greb family—Maaaa Greb. And by "scaled," it can be assumed he meant "stayed in my great aunt's riaaaad in Marrakech." That was back in 2014. Who knows, maybe this turn of phrase, which subsequently became lore among my group of friends at university, was the seed for my plan to ~~scale the Maghreb~~ go to Morocco myself. O how me and dead Mr Battutah chuckled.

There's no evidence that this is the great Tangerine's true resting place, just as Santiago de Compostela does not hold the bones of Saint James. Not that this in any way diminishes the pilgrim's endeavour. The hoards will continue to amass on the plains, and God bless them, for I would soon be a pilgrim too. If the idea is strong enough, it may as well be true.

At least there is no such thing, at least not yet, as the Camino de Ibn Battutah. Perhaps Morocco could well benefit, like all of us, from a bit more devotion through motion. Al-haraka baraka—the excellent Arabic saying that can mean anything from the literal "movement is a blessing" to the frustrated "get off your arse."

A few switchbacks from the tomb, I found myself in the creeping nausea of an Artists' Quarter, and an overpoweringly bohemian man launched himself from a doorstep:

"Matisse painted this door," he said, following me with gestures, "Jim Morrison bought these sandals."

A dark red djellaba swished about his ankles as he shuffled closer.

"You're in the former hippy capital of the world. Stop frowning!" he said, matching my step and reaching for my hand.

The man had a point, so I stopped, sat on his step, and listened. Abdullah had been a circus acrobat in Germany until he fell from the top of a human pyramid and broke his back. Now he loiters in the kasbah, stark like the metaphor he is, launching a photo of him and Jim Morrison at unsuspecting tourists. He called after me as I wandered off to some other café:

"Be happy!"

I met Soufian at the Syrian Mosque, where he sat with Roi from Israel and Lea from Germany. We talked until late over large helpings of beans, sharing stories and comparing tents. Travelling millennials ladened with vacant optimisms. All of us almosting it. But I was only half listening, eyes now set on the next stage.

Sometime in the small hours, I stood alone on the roof under a sky strewn with stars. The half-moon was at its first quarter, and the wind was blowing towards the Mediterranean. Boy, the neighbourhood did smell. Perhaps, at that very minute, a few unseasonal painted lady butterflies were fluttering above my head, preparing to fly north to England.

In that moment, I thought of Soufian, forever upbeat, working nights at a factory near an airport named after the world's greatest traveller. Far-flung dreams with hosting his only means. Folding distance through encounter like the Sufi.

I thought of Mohammed, the fisherman by the river, who'd traipsed the land in search of something he ultimately never found—living out his days on the dunes, watching the tides and laughing at the wind.

I thought of all the people in between, for each of the twenty-seven walking (forty-five total) days along one thousand kilometres of coastline. The dreams and the apathy. Tahhadi—challenge.

At the end of his book *Agadir*, Mohammed Khair-Eddine writes that he'll leave his country with only a poem in his pocket, and that's enough. For me, it was onwards along the butterfly tread. Four and a half months on a haphazard succession of routes to England. Europe just a short hop across the strait, to be hopped with a head full of memories that would take years to distil, be lost and then lovingly cherished. But I have my poem, and that is enough. It was my Moroccan journey; there are others.

SO THAT WAS THEN AND THIS IS NOW

"I have nothing uncommon to take notice of in my passage through France."

Daniel Defoe, *Robinson Crusoe*

"HOW DO?" SUGGESTED A dog walker near the Somerset Levels, "Where to with that bag?"

"Taunton."

"Come far?"

"Morocco."

"Proper job."

"Cheers then."

—

In the vast pine forests of Les Landes, south of Bordeaux, I met a shaman who told me that I was destined for failure in the next five years, but I'd find my life's true purpose on my fiftieth birthday. What to do in the meantime? Twenty years of baths and peanut butter sandwiches?

The Camino de Santiago is just as happily resigned to my memory as it is to midwinter. Warm hearts and hearths at every shiver. Truisms of hospitality confirmed true and frequently at the bottom of a bottle of home brew.

What began in Morocco as a trip full of vagrancy ended in stifling certainty, as these things do. All for one week of zen-like calm. But then, an anxious mind looks for something to be anxious about. That's not why I walked. I walked simply for the sake of walking. With feet as a vessel for encounter. And because it's fun.

The final detail was on my front door. Something I'd never noticed before, here at Camino's end, our knocker is a Santiago scallop shell. I arrived home to Brexit on the radio and unseasonal mince pies in the oven. That first night in bed, I dreamt I'd failed on the first day, stopped by police. Agadir was now no more than an ocean between the distant waves.

A few weeks later, I spoke at my sister's school to a class of seven-year-olds. I was introduced as an "adventurer." We talked about the   goats,   the   dogs,   the   food,   what "perseverance" means (and how to spell it), we danced, we tried on kit. And then a boy with red hair, who'd sat quietly throughout, raised a hand (gingerly):

"Your walk, do you regret it?"

I faltered for a second, gasped and gulped, my mind racing for what to say—I'm no adventurer, I just did a thing, and now I can't find a job. In a moment of clarity, I gathered myself and replied, "no," but what I meant was, "bollocks." And then I rode off to marry the Sunrise.

ACKNOWLEDGEMENTS

I'm forever grateful for my parents' limitless and endless encouragement (whether it's wild swimming with my mum or wild editing with my dad). My sister, Lizzie, a model for living a life of relentless positivity. Duncan (sorry for putting the flowers upside down at your wedding). Yacine for a keen take on things and for once trudging across Amman in the snow to bring me a kettle. Mohammed by the river for wearing a green jumper. Shoroq, bookending. And everyone else in between who lent an ear or an eye and, more importantly, the hundreds who housed me, fed me and watered me: those who are here, gone or never were.

James Scanlan is an Arabic-to-English translator from the UK based in Egypt.

www.james-scanlan.com

Photos from the trip:

amoroccanjourney.wordpress.com